To/ Jack

Alf Goldberg

June 2005

FROM WORLD'S END
TO WORLD WAR

In the sequel to his critically acclaimed memoir *World's End for Sir Oswald*, lifelong socialist Alf Goldberg translates his struggles against Oswald Mosley's fascists in London in the 1930s on to the global canvas of the fight against Nazism in the Second World War. From war-weary West London to West Lancashire and West Africa, from the Golden Mile to the Gold Coast—via barrage balloons, the merry wartime maelstrom of Blackpool and a nightmarish 4,000-mile voyage on a troopship—he recounts how his R.A.F. experiences reinforced the beliefs which had been forged during his impoverished upbringing in the "Threadbare Thirties". Moving accounts of solidarity and camaraderie are juxtaposed with descriptions of colonial racism and class frictions in a book that combines humour, tragedy, pathos and sharply observed social comment in equal measure. This compelling, starkly truthful account will appeal to local readers, political devotees, military history enthusiasts and ex-servicemen and women alike.

A former Labour councillor on Fylde Borough Council, Alf Goldberg is president of Blackpool and Fylde Trades Union Council, a leading campaigner for pensioners' rights and an active member of the Co-operative Party.

ALSO BY ALF GOLDBERG

World's End for Sir Oswald: Portraits of
Working-Class Life in Pre-War London

FROM WORLD'S END
TO WORLD WAR

A socialist serviceman's story

Alf Goldberg

Edited by Barry McLoughlin

The Progressive Press,
Lancashire

First published 2003

The Progressive Press,
46 Chain Lane,
Staining,
Lancashire,
FY3 0DD.

e-mail: barrymac@ukip.co.uk

Printed in Great Britain by Antony Rowe Ltd, Chippenham,Wiltshire

Cover design by Barry McLoughlin based on a 1941 souvenir programme for Blackpool Tower and Winter Gardens

British Library Cataloguing-in-Publication Data
A catalogue record for this book is available from the British Library

ISBN 0 9546121 0 8

CONTENTS

Foreword by TONY BENN

ALF Goldberg's latest book covering his experience in the second war is a truly wonderful one and anyone of that generation—of which I am one—will identify with it immediately.

Having met Mosley as a very young boy, when he was a Labour MP, seen him on the streets in his Blackshirt uniform in 1935, attended a meeting with my Dad in the East End broken up by the fascists, and having lived in North Kensington when he stood as a candidate in 1959, the many references to him in this book make a lot of sense.

More than that, having served in the R.A.F. as an "A.C.2", training to be pilot, in Rhodesia, I can confirm the meticulous accuracy of Alf Goldberg's account of service life which he describes with a splendid combination of wit and precision.

Those war years shaped the thinking of a whole generation, and the bureaucracy and absurdity of the military discipline within which we had to live in no way obscured the very serious discussions that took place amongst us. The British establishment and the Officer class were fighting another war against the Huns to teach them another lesson, but we were fighting fascism and although that did provide a common purpose of a kind, we all knew that the pre-war Tories would have been quite happy to do a

1

deal with Hitler, and, in a way, might have preferred to have been fighting the Soviet Union.

I remember on my troopship going out to Africa we decided to ask permission to have a meeting on board to discuss war aims and this was only granted on the understanding that there would be no politics—a restriction we ignored.

And coming home in another troopship after the European war was over, we actually held a mock election, and the full impact of the political education that the war had given us emerged in the contributions made and in the outcome.

Alf has got the mood and the atmosphere absolutely right, and he explains one of the most important factors that won Labour its post-war landslide victory, which was that we were all agreed there could be no going back to the 1930s, to unemployment, fascism, the means test and re-armament.

It was also obvious to everyone that if we could have full employment to kill people, we could have full employment to rebuild Britain by building hospitals, schools and libraries, and that planning for peace was just as necessary as planning for war.

Alf is a perfect example of the spirit of that generation, the ones who suffered in the 1930s—which I did not—who won the war and provided the political will for the Welfare State and the N.H.S., and all that the Attlee Government did, not least the dismantling of the Empire without the bloodshed that was experienced by the French in their resistance to decolonisation in Algeria and Vietnam.

Now the work of Alf and his comrades is systematically dismissed as Old Labour, but the younger generation are asking themselves the same questions about the injustice of global capitalism, and the international peace movement is as significant today as were the progressive anti-fascists of those far-off days before the war.

I have read quite a few wartime memoirs by those who served but this is in a different class because it opens up the real world of war—ninety per cent boredom, moments of real danger and endless opportunities to talk with others and think about the future.

I sense something of the same happening among those who are politically active today, and this is as good a textbook for them as you could find, and also a lot of fun to read.

Tony Benn,
London,
September 2003

INTRODUCTION

WAR, we are told, is both a great social leveller and a powerful national unifier; and so it frequently is. Certainly, during much of the Second World War, the pervasive spirit of fraternity, camaraderie and co-operation concreted across the cracks, albeit crudely, in a British nation that had been riven by economic and social injustices. Class barriers were blurred or even, sometimes, demolished as greater social cohesion was generated by the common struggle. Yet war and its shared suffering could also hide—or even heighten—these divisions, as exemplified more recently by the rift in British public opinion over the invasion of Iraq by the self-proclaimed coalition of the U.S.A. and Britain.

In the first volume of these memoirs, Alf Goldberg described movingly how his upbringing as a young man from a Jewish family amid the poverty of the World's End area of London had shaped his political outlook for the rest of his life. This sequel covers his experiences with the R.A.F. during the Second World War. It deals with both dimensions of war—the unifying and the divisive—and examines how the conflict further moulded and reinforced the political beliefs he had developed in the 1930s in the fight against Mosley and his British Union of Fascists.

It's perhaps appropriate that the most accurate description of the 1930s should have been coined by Marx—though it wasn't, of course, Karl. It was Groucho Marx who labelled the decade "The Threadbare Thirties", and how right he was. Alf Goldberg was determined that after the war we should never revisit those times, and this determination has been the motive force behind his political outlook for sixty years since then, as a socialist and trades unionist.

With his comrades, he experienced nearly six years of war from the unglamorous, gritty, grassroots perspective of the rank and file; there was little glory but plenty of guts, fear and perseverance, as they witnessed intolerance, snobbery and racism along with the solidarity, collectivism and sense of common endeavour.

In wartime the uniforms, unlike many civilians' clothes and the establishment's ideology, were rarely threadbare, but there were plenty of other problems and irritants to contend with. There was the petty tyranny of some of the N.C.O.s, as they inflicted degrading indignities on the "Erks", and the lofty aloofness of some of the officers. Imagination was frowned upon by many of Alf's "superiors", and innovation was stifled by the rigid regulations and bureaucracy. Mindless adherence to minor but absurdly rigid rules, and the harsh penalties that accompanied any infringements, fostered not discipline but disdain. War didn't just demand a massive physical cost in terms of human life and destruction of property; it also enervated the soul, and devalued education, learning, art and everything else that makes us fully human.

Class divisions did become less visible, and the ostentation that had been the hallmark of many upper-class Britons in the 1930s was anathematised as the nation slipped into "austerity" mode. Nowhere had this conspicuous consumption been more visible than in Alf Goldberg's own borough of Chelsea where, with apparent insouciance, unimaginable wealth coexisted alongside grinding poverty. War changed that … up to a point.

Overseas, however, relations between classes and races remained pretty much the same. During his service with the R.A.F. in West Africa he witnessed the crude, almost casual, racism that was a legacy of British imperialism. At around the same time, a young R.A.F. officer called Anthony Wedgwood Benn was encountering similar experiences on the opposite side of the continent, while training as a pilot in Southern Rhodesia.

At home, this clash of classes and cultures was most pointedly illustrated by the evacuation of hundreds of thousands of city children to safer areas at the start of the war. For the first time, evacuation saw upper and middle-class country families encounter the realities of life as lived by urban children.

Partly out of the need for self-preservation, the ruling classes soon realised that the appalling inequalities of the pre-war scene would become even less supportable if worsened by the wartime shortages. And, after a shaky start, the rationing system did begin to provide a rough-and-ready equality—albeit one that could usually be overcome on the black market if you had the cash. Those with more money than conscience were still able to circumvent the clothing restrictions, for example: household furnishings were initially coupon-free, and the less fastidious among the wealthy soon discovered a hitherto unsuspected fondness for chair covers made of Harris tweed. When the Government imposed a five shilling limit on hotel meals, the price of post-prandial coffee, which was not controlled, rose astronomically—a cynically effective way of ensuring the restaurants retained their upper-crust clientele.

The inevitable shortages of basic items also contributed to another of the less savoury, and less celebrated, aspects of wartime life: the increase in crime. "Spivs", racketeers, black marketeers and old-fashioned gangsters were quick to exploit the wartime opportunities. As late as 1950, in the so-called "Blackpool Rock Racket", a group of spivs was arrested after being caught selling the resort's most famous product without sweet coupons.

However, there were always those who "did well out of the war" while remaining on the right side of the law. Just as in the Great War, there were the "hard-faced men" for whom it provided a profitable business opportunity. And as a socialist, Alf Goldberg was torn between two competing imperatives: to fight the spread of European fascism, and to resist being sucked into another war over capital, in which the only losers would be the working classes of the combatant countries. His hatred of fascism was such that the former won the battle for his conscience. But this didn't mean that he and his comrades lost sight of the long-term aim of the war: not just to defeat Nazism but to build a better society on the foundations laid during those six grim years.

Alf and his comrades were also fighting the hunger and hopelessness, unemployment and ill education, that had blighted the lives of so many of his contemporaries from the World's End. In demanding a clarification of the war aims of the Government, the labour movement was looking beyond the end of the conflict to the social aims of a post-war Britain. They certainly weren't fighting the war to be unemployed or badly housed again. As the *Daily Herald* asked: "Are we fighting to preserve Carlton Gardens and the Savoy while we return to the slums?" Would the enforced egalitarianism of war be replaced by a return of malnutrition? And if all men were equal before God and the bomber, why couldn't they be more equal in the daily business of living?

The living standards of many working-class people rose during the war and for the first time they were enjoying full and regular employment. The necessary austerity was unpleasant, but gave millions a better standard of nutrition and clothing than in peacetime. It was not yet a case of "many who are first will be last", as in the New Testament parable, but at least the last were a little closer to the first on the economic and social stepladder. As the *Herald* put it: "There was no longer the obscene comparison between the conditions of the unemployed and the extravagances of the wealthy. The unemployed became employed and were able to afford their rations, whilst the wealthy were curbed both by the organisation of controls and the strength of public opinion." Women, too, were liberated from the drudgery of domestic life as they moved into jobs vacated by their conscripted menfolk. But what would happen when Britain stopped building bombers and battleships?

Thankfully, the Labour members of the War Cabinet were already pondering these questions, and the Beveridge Plan, published as early as December 1942, proposed the first comprehensive national framework of social security. Only by pursuing long-term aims such as this would Britons be able to ensure that the collective euphoria of V.E. Day and V.J. Day did not evaporate into the inequitable free-for-all that had characterised British society before the war. For the crowds gathered outside Buckingham Palace and in thousands of town centres across the nation, there was to be no going back to "The Threadbare Thirties".

Barry McLoughlin,
Editor

8

CHAPTER ONE

Folks who never did live on a hill

One day we'll build a home on a hilltop high,
You and I ... And we'll be pleased to be called...
The folks who live on the hill.

TRAGICALLY, many of my friends and contemporaries in the ramshackle World's End area of West London in 1939, when this popular and poignant ballad was being sung, were never to savour the tender contentment evoked by its lyrics. Indeed, although they did not know it at the time, they were never destined to. These young men would shortly be issued with rifles and uniforms many of which, ironically, predated the Second World War by more than two decades. As I was later able to confirm myself, some of these supposedly "new" uniforms still bore the dates verifying their manufacture during the Great War. History was repeating itself, but both times as tragedy.

This sweetly optimistic song was the party-piece of my good friend Victor. We all had our favourite tunes, and there were many opportunities to sing them at a time when it was obvious that preparations for war were being made, generating an undercurrent of uncertainty and apprehension of the unknown. These feelings of foreboding were particularly marked, of course, among those who were likely to be the first to be involved in the coming conflict. Standing in the rain at Heston Airport in 1938, the Prime Minister, Neville Chamberlain, waved his much-vaunted piece of paper, signed by Herr Hitler, promising "peace in our time" on his return from Munich. Few of us young folk believed his message and we certainly had no desire to be associated with a so-called peace that involved the summary annexation of land on the continent of Europe which was being perpetrated almost daily by the German fascist army.

Although Victor and I were good friends, we did not have the same background, he being still at college while I was earning a sparse living in the motor trade as a mechanic. I suppose I was more streetwise, and he did not particularly share my friendships with those who had the same socialist political aspirations as myself. Nevertheless, our friendship was strong, though it was more associated with affairs of the heart, as we courted two sisters from the same family—Dolly and Rose. It was usual for World's End families in those days to be large. Our fiancées' was no exception, comprising four brothers and five sisters.

Victor and I were unaware of it at the time, but those few idyllic summer months in 1939, which we were to spend with them all and which brought so much happiness, would—thanks to the awful vicissitudes of war—never be recaptured. This happiness was not derived from any expensive or exotic means but merely from the mundane, quotidian pursuits by which the working class of the day enjoyed themselves. At the weekend the whole family would journey *en bloc* by public transport the few miles out to Wimbledon Common from Chelsea. There, they would picnic, and play games of cricket, football or rounders; everyone, irrespective of age or physical ability, participated with gusto and glee but with varying levels of achievement.

During the day ample refreshment would be guaranteed, particularly by Joe, a son-in-law, who being a plumber always succeeded in the arduous task of transporting his blow lamp and tea urn on these outings. In the evenings, the revelry was continued when the whole assembly retreated to the beer garden of a nearby pub, where they would consume their ale and softer drinks and sing their Cockney songs, before a not-so-comfortable bus journey back to Chelsea in the darkness of the late evening, exhausted but content. For them, those outings could best be described in that moving verse by the poet Thomas Gray in his *Elegy Written in a Country Churchyard:*

> Let not Ambition mock their useful toil,
> Their homely joys, and destiny obscure;
> Nor Grandeur hear with a disdainful smile
> The short and simple annals of the poor.

Both Victor and I were happy to be accepted into the heart of this large family and there was no question in our minds that we would eventually both share homes with our fiancées, on possibly a "hilltop high" exactly as he used to sing about. But, alas, few aspirations were to come to fruition. With the seasons' transition following that summer, through the autumn into the early winter, so simultaneously the whole fabric of our lives began to change at an ever-increasing rate. Although we were still at the stage of the so-called "Phoney War", actual conflict was inevitable, and the build-up was accordingly manifest. Contemporaries, lifelong friends and acquaintances were leaving the fold for a multitude of reasons. Some, already officers and N.C.O.s in the Territorial Army, were eagerly joining as regulars to secure the initial advantage of their existing ranks. Others, who were not enamoured of the military and were skilled tradesmen, were leaving to fill well-paid exempt positions with the contractors who had obtained lucrative armaments contracts in many parts of the country. My friend Victor had little problem deciding his near future, having arranged to complete his college studies before entering the R.A.F. as a trainee pilot.

For me and my streetwise friends, things were not so straightforward. Like our parents, we were seeing ourselves again involved in a war over capital, a system which had given our class a criminally minor share of its spoils. Our dilemma was that this time it was the extreme right in the form of European fascism that we could see was the enemy. Having in recent times been active in the fight against British fascism in the form of Oswald Mosley's party, the British Union of Fascists, our political education was such that we were fully aware of the necessity of eradicating the evil of European fascism. This awareness would inevitably sweep aside any objections to the looming hostilities.

Inexorably it happened: at 11.15am on September 3 1939 the Prime Minister announced on the radio from 10 Downing Street the declaration of war with Germany as Hitler's troops marched into Poland. It was just a few hours later, as I was walking the short distance between my home in the World's End and my girlfriend Dolly's house, that the first air raid warning siren sounded. It seemed that in a few seconds everyone disappeared, leaving me alone in the streets! Being halfway to my destination, I hurried (actually, of course, I ran) through the deserted streets to the house in Uverdale Road, but, despite many repeated loud bangings on the door knocker, I met with no response. It soon became obvious that, with the exception of myself, everyone in the neighbourhood had swiftly decamped to their backyard Anderson shelters. I sat down on the front doorstep of the four-storey terraced house, from which there was no access to the safety of the rear Anderson shelter, bewildered by the intensity of the silence. I awaited fearfully my baptism to the awful cacophony of shrieking shells and falling bombs that I had associated with sudden warfare, convinced that this would really be my kismet. However, after what seemed a very long 15 minutes, my trepidation was to be interrupted by the shattering wailing of a siren, my first experience of the joy of hearing an all-clear.

As the people began to appear through the front doors and pour into the streets, we did not realise that this experience was to herald the start of a few months of what could almost be described as an enjoyable war, when the streets would be at peace, free from troubled skies and wailing sirens. Many celebrations and parties (knees-ups) would be held, to greet the fathers, sons and sisters who arrived home on leave or to bid farewell to those who would be called to destinations that many previously never knew existed. I can recall an occasion in the local bar when, after deliberations over a fellow toper's posting to Fazakerley, it was decided that, as it was a place unheard of by anyone present, it must be overseas. After all, as Cockneys I suppose they could be excused for not knowing a suburb of Liverpool!

Although this peaceful period was to be but the prelude, in a few short months, to one of the worst tragedies ever to befall a great city, it also heralded a spirit for good. It fostered a friendship among people that was to grow into a form of brotherhood and permeated all classes of society. For more than half a decade, it was to be something of a social "equaliser" (although the pundits from the previous campaigns, in the saloon bars, were assuring us youngsters that "it would be all over in a few weeks"). We who lived through those times would never forget an experience that eventually—and, perhaps, inevitably—was to disappear whenever peace prevailed, heralding the re-emergence of life in a capitalist society once again.

CHAPTER TWO
June 1940

THE breathtaking speed of the events taking place at this time found me married to Dolly with a newly-born baby son and employed in an "exempt from military service" job, repairing ambulances for the A.R.P. (Air Raid Precautions), although we were still in the honeymoon period prior to the air raids that were to blitz London.

Political events were moving equally rapidly. As a socialist, I had long been an admirer of Clement Attlee, the diffident, laconic but incongruously passionate leader of the Labour Party. In the immediate post-war years, his Government was to lay the foundations for a social and economic transformation of Britain that would liberate millions of working people from the fears of unemployment, destitution and poor education and health. But "Major Attlee", a Gallipoli veteran and East End MP, was also a staunch patriot and in May 1940 led the Labour Party into the wartime coalition with Churchill following the resignation of the well-intentioned but hapless Chamberlain (though it was to be nearly another two years before he was formally styled "Deputy Prime Minister"). Showing characteristic political astuteness, Attlee—who knew his party well—made sure he received the endorsement of the Labour conference in Bournemouth immediately after his key meeting with Churchill on membership of the

War Cabinet. Attlee's detractors (who had at one time included Churchill) frequently mistook his incommunicative character for weakness: as the war and his 1945-51 Government demonstrated, however, there was iron in his soul. His apparently bourgeois habits and personal conservatism sheathed the steely blade of a determined radicalism, forged by his encounters with poverty in the East End in the 1920s.

Unsurprisingly, Attlee was also dismissive of his former colleague, Oswald Mosley, with whom he had debated at the Cambridge Union in early 1933. The British fascist movement was "really Mosley and nothing more," he wrote after the debate. "He has not any coherent ideas."

In May 1940 Germany invaded Holland and Belgium, and three weeks after Labour joined the Government, Britain's exhausted and demoralised troops were being plucked from the beaches at Dunkirk. In June Marshal Pétain's new French Government asked Hitler for an armistice, and Britain stood alone to face a summer of bombing and what seemed almost certain invasion. The "Phoney War" was over.

At this time I was still working in the Fulham Road, living with Dolly in a nearby flat in what would today be described in house agents' parlance as "a desirable area". Having seen the "to let" sign at the front of the house, I approached the owner, who was decorating the flat on the first floor, and asked about the rent. On receiving the reply "fifteen shillings a week" I turned abruptly to descend the stairs, remarking: "Sorry, too dear." Then he leaned over the banisters and shouted down: "You can have it for twelve shillings and sixpence," to which I immediately responded: "You're on!"

This was rather cavalier of me in view of the fact that the flat was unfurnished, and I had neither furniture, furnishings nor the wherewithal to provide them. In fact, however, this was to prove little problem as within seven days Dolly, the baby and I were comfortably installed, complete with bedroom and kitchen furniture, furnishings and floor-coverings, by courtesy of the Times Furnishing Company Ltd. The promptness of this action was aided by the fact that I dealt with the servicing of the local branch manager's car and by the system of "easy payments". The latter was known in some quarters as the "glad I got it, sorry I can't pay" system. This was not so very far from the truth in my case, as the financial transaction was not to be completed for six years—"after hostilities"—circumstances over which I was unfortunately to have no control. We had not been installed in this very comfortable flat for more than a few weeks when I received notification to attend a medical examination and a trade test prior to enlistment in the R.A.F. This presented me with something of a dilemma.

Victor had now started his training course as a pilot in the R.A.F. Likewise, it seemed that all my friends and acquaintances had disappeared into the various services and other wartime activities. Even my father, who was over fifty and had served throughout the First World War—and had been discharged as medically unfit, with a pension, two decades earlier—had rejoined his Royal Engineers regiment, classified "A1"! My

17

mother had left their World's End flat to follow him to Derby, where he was stationed. Dolly's family still lived a couple of miles from us in Chelsea, although some of her brothers had been called up into the military. As yet, however, the area had not experienced any of the terror that was to be inflicted upon it and its people within the next few months by the *Luftwaffe*.

What should I do? I had the "exemption from service" papers that my employer had given me to use in this anticipated circumstance. Should I attend for examination but refrain from producing the papers and thus go through the procedure that would result in my acceptance of the King's Shilling or, in this case, the R.A.F.'s "two bob a day"? My detestation of the Nazis and my desire to continue to be active in the fight against fascism won the day. I duly presented myself for examination without any exemption papers being produced.

On the day I was happy to be included among those dozens of other lithe young men who, stripped of their clothing and subjected to a thorough communal examination, were declared physically "A1" fit. However, I soon realised along with my examination officer that my theoretical knowledge of engineering was not to the standard required by the R.A.F. Although I was accepted, I would be required to attend a sixteen-week course after the initial six-week disciplinary course at R.A.F. Cardington, in Bedfordshire. Of course, my next problem was to inform my employer of this arrangement. This I had planned to do later, at the appropriate time—which would be when I had plucked up the courage!

It was just a couple of weeks later that I received the inevitable summons, complete with instructions and rail ticket for the journey to Bedford, for the start of my R.A.F. service at Cardington. So great was my desire and determination by this time to be positively involved in the immense changes which were unfolding that I decided to tell my employer of the imminent loss of my services at the last possible moment, to prevent him taking any action to thwart my wishes.

It was therefore on a lovely summer's day in June 1940 that I entered his office with great apprehension to tell him that the next day, the 16th (like his service number, no serviceman could ever forget this enlistment date), I would no longer be a civilian. He shouted something like "Hang on—there's something wrong here somewhere!" as he simultaneously grabbed for the telephone, during which time I hastily retreated from the room. Sadly, I never did see him again as it would have been nice at some time to have apologised for my shabby treatment of him.

The next day was to remain memorable for me as I shared in the uncertainties and partings that frequently befell family life in those times. Particularly in my case did I realise for the first time the trauma of leaving a young wife and baby alone to face the vagaries of a war. My sorrow would have been deepened if I had known at the time the horror that was to fall from the air in the near future upon London.

So it was with a great feeling of despondency that I walked across the footbridge at King's Cross Station and looked down on the platform where I was to board the special train for Bedford. It was obviously to be for the exclusive use of servicemen as already many groups of young men, with their multifarious articles of baggage, were assembling on the platform. As I looked down upon them, it seemed to me that even then friendships were being formed, as they sought to overcome the acute feelings of unexpectancy, isolation and sheer loneliness that they were experiencing. Little did I realise that I myself was about to form a real friendship on that very train which would endure for many years to come.

But a most important thing I was about to learn was the inherent humour that was always generated collectively whenever a body of men were gathered. Indeed, the wit that manifested itself was to have a major influence on our eventual victory in the conflict. Paramount also was the respect I was to learn later for the exceptional knowledge, education and wisdom of some friends I made in the Air Force; most, I hasten to record, were men who in the eyes of the services and wider society would be considered to be of the lowest common denominator, never bothering to try to win promotion.

When I arrived on the platform, walking among the many small groups, excitement tinged with bravado permeated the armosphere. The majority of those present were from the London area, whereas later a greater mixture of young men from across the land with different cultures would be banded together. With the arrival of the train, it would have appeared to an observer that many lifelong friendships had been cemented, for, amid much clamour and banter, carriages were quickly filled and seats commandeered on behalf of friends who had been unknown but a brief time beforehand. There must have been some parochialism involved as I remember considering my new-found friend Ronnie, who hailed from Hammersmith, not being such a true-blue Londoner as myself, Chelsea being at least three miles nearer Westminster! Certainly these—for the most part exuberant—young men were not to know that this would be the last day for almost six years that they would legally be allowed to wear their civilian clothes and, indeed, such is the nature of war, that some would be discarding them for ever.

Arriving at R.A.F. Cardington, having been transferred there from Bedford railway station by trucks, I experienced my first example of the humour I always found whenever troops were assembled. Having arrived in an empty courtyard, a loud voice was heard inquiring from a crowded truck: "What! No reception committee?" This, however, was to be the last undisciplined remark ventured during the next six weeks. We were to find our stay at Cardington little different from serving "six weeks' hard" in Wormwood Scrubs.

That first evening was to prove a rude introduction to our future service life. Having received a meal and still in our comfortable civilian clothes and in possession of the proceeds of our final civilian pay packets, we took the opportunity of invading the N.A.A.F.I. bars at their evening opening. For a couple of hours ale was consumed rapidly at the convenient price of fourpence per pint, after which it appeared to us that this was to be a lovely war. However, when the party was beginning to go with a swing and approaching its height, much to the consternation of the revellers it ended abruptly at 9pm. This was brought about by three simultaneous events. First, the turning out of the lights, then the slamming shut of the bar shutters, followed by a corporal jumping on a bar table and demanding raucously: "Get out!". This made a distinct impression on everyone present as to the power possessed even by the lowliest N.C.O.—even at times, it would seem later, the power to decide between life and death!

At this period in 1940 the number of recruits entering the R.A.F. was very great, which was resulting in rapid promotion for the regular time-serving members, mostly "ex-boy service", who in peacetime would have had little chance of reaching the dizzy heights of the non-commissioned officers. They were therefore happy to inflict upon the unfortunate "sprogs" beneath them the same harsh treatment that they had endured from their superiors during the years since they themselves were "sprogs". (This latter sobriquet, which in the R.A.F. was used to describe a recruit with only a short period of service, had an amusing origin. Apparently during a recruit's first engineering trade test he was shown a gear wheel. He was asked, "What is it?" to which he replied: "A sprog". He had been nervously confused between a cog and a sprocket!)

Following the evening of our rude awakening into the life we could expect to lead as an "A-C Plonk" in the R.A.F. came some early days which alternated between rich humour and downright pathos. The kitting-out process prompted humour that was all the more pointed by its being completely unintentional. Complaints during this exercise were rife but useless. Imagine the look of incredulity on the face of someone who, having complained that the vests issued to him were too big, was informed that they would "shrink in the wash". But when he complained "the pants are too tight", he was told they would "stretch as you wear them"!

R.A.F. personnel at this time were privileged to be issued with more comfortable jackets than the dog-collared varieties that had been in use some years earlier; they had lapels allowing a tie and collared shirt to be worn, alleviating the roughness of a tunic collar. However, stores supplies could not always keep up with the enormous demand, so it was necessary that old stock be delved into to satisfy the increase in enlistment. Inevitably this resulted in a few recruits being unfortunate in the luck of the draw and receiving an old issue of a dog-collared tunic. This happened to one member of my entry who, despite his immediate protests, was unable to have it changed. Later, back in the billet, he was almost reduced to tears when it was discovered the tunic bore a tag revealing that it had been made in 1918—two years before he was born. As I indicated in chapter one, the fact that a civilised society could be issuing military garments to a young man that could have been made for his father, to do battle in a previous war, was an irony not lost on most of the "sprogs" present.

The weather during that 1940 summer was to prove marvellous and, although the next six weeks' training was to seem little different from doing "porridge" in the Scrubs, the humour that was always endemic among those very fit and exuberant young men helped us to enjoy a semblance of a normal life. This was perhaps most apparent in the dining rooms, although at times they inspired more antagonistic emotions. One of my first unfortunate experiences was to be randomly chosen for cookhouse duties. This initially proved quite pleasant as it involved ladling salad (mostly lettuce) from huge bowls on to the plates of the hungry lads as they filed past me, still sweating from their gruelling drill and physical training routines. Some were requesting extra ladles of tomatoes, cucumbers and onions rather than lettuce, and I was dutifully obliging. This was abruptly interrupted by a duty sergeant's heavy hand pulling me from the tables, as he growled: "Where do you think you are—bloody Lyon's Corner House?" I was then demoted to the kitchen area and those sacks of potatoes piled to the ceiling, given a knife and ordered to "get peeling!" It was the first and last time that I was ever to savour that awful experience in my entire R.A.F. career. I made a point of seeing to that.

On another occasion I overheard a conversation in the dining room that was to typify the chicanery and hypocrisy that often characterised the attitudes of the military hierarchy to the lower ranks. My squad was seated six to a table in the dining room and about to begin the evening meal when we suddenly became aware of a group of officers advancing along the centre aisle of the dining room towards us and stopping next to our table. Unusually, we had also noticed there were large tables along the opposite wall, laden with food. Although we were aware that things were not "normal", we were not party to the fact that we were in the presence of royalty. We quickly recognised the uniformed officer heading the group as being no less a personage than a younger brother of the King, George VI, and of the former (and only briefly reigning) King Edward VIII. Being well within earshot, I was dumbfounded when the prince asked the leading officer, "What is the food doing on those tables opposite?" and received the reply, "That is for the trainees, sir, if they request further helpings." You could not possibly imagine those hungry young men's appetites being satisfied by the sparse rations supplied at their evening meal and then "not" requesting further helpings! Although the answer did seem to satisfy the prince, he may well have asked it with his tongue in his cheek. At least no-one later had the guts to go over and help themselves to "further helpings", not even those at our table who had overheard the conversation. Needless to record, these tables laden with food never appeared again.

Eventually one of the longest four weeks in the new recruits' lives came to an end and we were offered parole for a weekend, from 17.00 hours on Friday until 23.59 hours on Sunday. Very few of the intake did not take advantage of this short escape to freedom and sanity. Fortunately the lad with the twenty-two-year-old dog-collared tunic was able to borrow a modern jacket from a mate (who could not take advantage of the respite and was staying in camp): he had vowed never to go home and greet his mother in a garment that could have been issued to his late father, who had not survived the previous war.

Armed with a rail warrant to London, I shared the elation of my fellow "sprogs" on that train as we travelled back to meet our loved ones even for such a short spell. On dispersal at Euston Station and joining the seething mass of humanity, however, I experienced an unexpected embarrassment due to having for the first time to acknowledge every officer encountered (they were very prevalent) with a salute. These feelings were to evaporate eventually when I was to convince myself—in accordance with what we were told by our superiors—that it was in fact the uniforms I was respecting rather than the wearers.

I know that there are two things my contemporaries will remember to the end of their days. As I wrote earlier, one is their regimental number (associated with so many pay parades) and the other their first short leave with their introduction to a leave form, hopefully accompanied by a free rail warrant. In my case (although I was not to realise it at the time) this first 48-hour leave pass would always, in addition, be remembered as the last time for some years that I was to spend at home with my family under a trouble-free sky. Shortly afterwards, the whole population of London and the other large British cities were to be the victims of the *Luftwaffe*'s blitzes, experiencing the unprecedented horrors of modern warfare.

Six weeks after arriving at Cardington, the kitting-out and the disciplinary courses completed, we were all destined to be posted on to our various further trade training courses across the U.K. and in some cases even farther afield. During those weeks, young men from all different walks and stations of life had been thrown together in an intimacy they could never have visualised, and many friendships that had been forged were to be broken. To some, it was very nearly a trauma: although they were not to know it at the time, it would be an emotion they would experience many times during the coming years.

For my part, along with many of my friends, we were to be posted to No. 8 School of Technical Training at R.A.F. Weeton, a camp in the countryside near Blackpool in Lancashire. This was considered to be a posting to the "Far North" by friends hailing from the South, most of us never having travelled further than Birmingham.

During the six weeks' training at Cardington, the officer in charge of discipline on our Wing was a former Indian Cavalry officer of the military old school who had presumably re-enlisted in the emergency at the outbreak of war. He was old enough to have seen service in the previous war. He was certainly a strict disciplinarian and this trait he had obviously brought with him from a previous age. This was not appreciated by the younger generation of recruits who resented him and considered him to be, in the parlance of the R.A.F. at the time, "filled with bullshit". So when it was known that he too would be posted to Weeton, to be in charge of the Wing's discipline at the camp, it was hardly a morale-booster for those involved. Personally, however, I respected him and considered him a character from an almost bygone age of the military establishment, even if he appeared to be something of an anachronistic "Colonel Blimp" figure to some of the men under his command.

During the time I was to be under his command, like all characters, he sometimes unintentionally generated jocularity through incidents in which he was involved and he certainly provided a butt for the lower ranks' irreverent jokes, as I shall record in the next chapter.

CHAPTER THREE

R.A.F. Weeton No. 8 School of Technical Training, 1940

IT WAS an evening in late August when we disembarked at Kirkham and Wesham railway station in Lancashire, midway between Preston and Blackpool and an important junction for the holiday trains to the resorts of the Fylde Coast. On the approach to Kirkham from Preston, we had seen on the left the anonymous sprawl and high fences of the government's weapons establishment at Salwick, which is today the Springfields plant of British Nuclear Fuels Ltd and now devoted, thankfully, to civil use. It had been a hot summer in the South but as we clambered on to the lorries *en route* for Weeton Camp, there was an autumnal chill in the air which was noticeable to those like me who had never been so far north before. My first impression of the area was, in the circumstances, a somewhat gloomy one. This feeling was not enhanced by the view, as we were driven away, of the first cotton mill that I had ever seen. Situated opposite the station, next to the railway tracks, in the fading evening light it certainly fitted my impression of Blake's "dark satanic mills". I did not know it at the time, but the textile industry in Kirkham had declined dramatically in the first half of the twentieth century, a decline accentuated by the town's position outside the mainstream of the cotton industry in its Pennine heartlands. Today there are no working textile mills and most of the buildings have been demolished. And, indeed, the building I saw opposite the station turned out to be no longer in use: the former mill, we were told, housed special German prisoners who were considered to be of high risk. Although in the future we were to pass this ex-mill many times, there was never evidence of any inmates. On these occasions, particularly in midwinter, I would feel compassion for anyone incarcerated for an indeterminate period in such a forbidding and foreboding building.

The settlement of Kirkham was a market town, granted its charter in 1287 in the reign of Edward I, but it was transformed into a factory town in the nineteenth century after the development of a large-scale flax trade. This allowed the wealthy local flax merchants to lay down the pattern of modern Kirkham with their impressive town houses built beside the elongated main street running east-west along a low ridge, with cottages for their workforce just off this main thoroughfare. The ridge was pretty modest in height but in terms of the flatness of most of the Fylde it was virtually vertiginous. Kirkham was linked to the less populous township of Wesham, which had once been a separate settlement, with a small industrial enclave serving the railway that since 1840 had bisected it.

R.A.F. Weeton was set in hundreds of acres of rural land some eight miles inland from Blackpool, Britain's best-known and most boisterous holiday resort. Like Blackpool itself, it was to become of vast importance to the R.A.F. throughout the war years, as a technical training school for most ground staff trades and even for aircrew eventually to "re-muster" to those trades. During those years hundreds of thousands of trainees passed these courses, which were based on shortened versions of the pre-war R.A.F. apprenticeships and therefore provided the high-class trade training so sorely needed, with a concentration on transport and its ancillary trades. Earlier it had been recognised that the R.A.F. needed a vast expansion of its road transport facilities, and Weeton met that need.

Weeton itself was a tiny, tranquil settlement midway between Blackpool and Kirkham, centred on a small triangular village green and the local pub, the Eagle and Child, one of the oldest in the Fylde, its age-worn beams marinated in centuries of tobacco smoke and beer fumes. The Eagle and Child was a popular haunt for R.A.F. men during the war, though the walk back to the camp down the darkened lane after a few drinks could prove to be something of a challenge. The railway crossed the south-western edge of Weeton village and there had, briefly, been a small halt there, but as this had closed almost a century earlier—in 1843—it was of somewhat academic interest in terms of our travelling arrangements.

Weeton was a former estate village of the Earls of Derby, Lords of the Manor from the seventeenth century, and was to be greatly expanded by housing in the 1960s and 1970s as it became a dormitory settlement for Blackpool and Preston. Just outside the centre of the village was its squat, early-Victorian brick-built parish church, St Michael's, with its low, louvred steeple over-shadowed by the trees surrounding it. Originally a chapel of its

31

namesake church at Kirkham, it was created in 1843 and is now 'semi-detached' from the main village by the M55.

The road up from the village green towards Kirkham leads to the site of the village's eighteenth-century windmill, just a few yards from the hurly-burly of the modern M55. Approached along a lane that was elegiacally eulogised by local historian (and veteran socialist) Allen Clarke, the fine tower mill and its cluster of associated buildings had once formed a thriving little community. By the early 1950s, however, it was considered to be in a dangerous condition and demolished—though it was so sturdily built that it took two steam engines to do the job. Today all that remains are the circular foundations of the mill, which after years as a patch of overgrown brickwork have now been attractively landscaped.

By the end of the 1700s, Weeton's was one of nearly 40 mills in the Fylde, an area dubbed by Clarke—author, poet, publisher, political polemicist and journalist—"Windmill Land" in his celebrated book of the same name in the early twentieth century. Born in poverty in Bolton, Clarke was a self-taught polymath who was familiar with Blackpool from the days when his family holidayed there. He had worked in the textile mills as an eleven-year-old but his life was transformed when he won a scholarship to Hulton Grammar School in Bolton. Later, he and his wife, Lila, became so enraptured by their cycle rides through the lanes of the Fylde that they decided to settle there. For Clarke, these vast slow-moving monoliths symbolised a more innocent, Arcadian era in comparison with the stygian murk and frenetic piecework of the Industrial Revolution. However, he was not an unreconstructed romantic, yearning for the false tranquillity of a mythical medieval England: Clarke was an avid advocate of socialism and a fierce critic of the ills of modern industrial society, which he had experienced directly as a boy back in the mills of his native Bolton.

The camp was about half a mile north of Weeton, on the winding road leading to its sister village of Singleton, and at its peak measured about three-quarters of a mile square. Its rambling sprawl of huts and hangars spilled across the main Weeton-Singleton road, though these days the site—now an Army camp—is much reduced. Ministry of Defence warning signs stand eerie sentinel on tracts of land that once echoed to the shouts and laughter of the "Erks", and the commands of their N.C.O.s. I did not, of course, know it at the time, but it is less than three miles from the village of Staining, where Dolly and I would subsequently make our home.

On arrival at camp we were the first entry to be installed in a vast, recently built arrangement of wooden structures comprising dormitories, bath houses, offices and all manner of differently designed huts, collectively known as "Number Four Wing". This Wing was to become our living quarters for the twelve weeks of the newly-arranged course; the training itself would be carried out in the technical training area across the camp. We were informed that the course would be referred to as "motor transport mechanic (M.T.M.) Group Two" and we were eventually to realise the importance of the "Group Two" suffix. In those days

R.A.F. trades were grouped from Nos. 1 to 5 according to the trade skills of the men. No. 1 group was considered the highest-skilled, down to No. 5 ranked the lowest. This system was connected to the pay structure which could result in big anomalies. It was possible for a Group Five senior N.C.O. (sergeant) only to receive the same pay as a Group One Leading Aircraftsman (L.A.C.). This could lead to animosity, particularly on Training Command stations like Weeton where, unfortunately, those responsible for discipline, drill instructors and those graded "general duties" personnel were designated Group Five, in contrast to the technical trades being mostly Group One. In addition, friction could be exacerbated by R.A.F. documents alluding to those designated Group Five as "Aircrafthands" and higher groups as "Aircraftsmen". This resulted in some sections referring to those they considered to be of a lower order than themselves as "I.B.A.s"—"ignorant bloody aircrafthands". But all this was of little interest to us at the time because, as just "A.C. plonks", our princely pay was two bob a day and, being paid fortnightly by the R.A.F., we received twenty-eight bob every pay parade. Incidentally, we soon learned to forget any thoughts of an early visit home as the return fare from Blackpool to London was twenty-eight bob and fourpence!

Life away from the technical areas, back in the Wing under the jurisdiction of the disciplinary regime, was characterised by its unnecessary parades, duties and rules, which, interpreted by mostly ignorant people, became downright stupid. The harshness and at times unfairness resulting from all this were accurately defined by us, its victims, by the all-embracing term "bullshit". As Weeton was a camp under the control of Training Command, its rules adhered strictly to the maxim: "If it moves, salute it—if it's stationary, paint it!"

During the early weeks of our course, an incident happened that alerted me to the level of intelligence that you could expect from those immediately in control of our destiny. Our course entry were billeted in the same hut, which consisted of thirty bed spaces and two small separate rooms at the end, one for an N.C.O. and the other used as a store. Unfortunately we were the victims one night of a prowler who took advantage of the soundness of our sleep to help himself to a couple of wallets. The next day, we were visited by the camp "S.P.s" (R.A.F. Special Police) comprising a flight sergeant and a corporal, who ordered every occupant to empty the contents of his kitbag on to his bed to enable the inspection of the items. This system, it seemed, was always adopted on these occasions, but never actually assisted the investigations. It was hardly likely that, if the culprit was indeed billeted in the hut, he would stash the swag in his own kitbag! I think that really it was an opportunity for the S.P.s to probe into the possibility of other misdemeanours being revealed.

On this occasion, however, the senior N.C.O., when he reached my bed, picked up a book entitled *German Fascism*, and ordered the corporal to confiscate it as he declared it to be "subversive material". He dismissed my pleas that its author, Professor Harold Laski, as an internationally-known anti-fascist, would be one of the first to be shot by Hitler, given the chance. Fortunately the corporal did not accede to the confiscation order, probably, I imagined, because he had a better knowledge of the current affairs of the time than his supposed superior.

Weeton Camp was ideally located for Training Command as that area of the North West was rarely subject to the attention of enemy aircraft, which allowed the training courses to proceed without interruption and was a great asset to the R.A.F. technical training programme. During the years of the heavy bombing of U.K. cities, however, much heartache was inflicted on those trainees whose homes and families were targets of the air raids. Leave was only granted in cases of extreme hardship, and rail chaos generally made journeys long and hectic. But the strong bonds of friendship and camaraderie forged between us all maintained spirits and kept up morale.

After a couple of months, our entry were beginning the second half of the course, and we were starting to consider ourselves to be case-hardened "Erks". At least we had acquired much more knowledge about our contemporaries and service life than we had set out with. Naturally most recruits had not taken kindly to the discipline of the "King's Rules", which appeared to them to be stupid and unnecessary. Responsibility for this was laid firmly at the door of the former Indian Army Cavalry officer who had accompanied us from the beginning. Their attitude was apparent when during a sports session he democratically arranged to take part himself in a hundred-yards race, handicapped according to age. Removing his officer's tunic, and being by far the oldest competitor, he strode to the front resplendent in his red

36

braces, whereupon a loud voice in a Cockney accent (and safe somewhere in the centre of another couple of hundred lads), much to the merriment of all, shouted: "Where's yer bleedin' horse!" As I said in the previous chapter, I considered him to be a character straight out of Britain's imperial past.

This was emphasised when I was picked to act as one of the two escorts for an unfortunate offender to be brought up in front of him on a charge. Procedure on these occasions was that the prisoner was flanked by the two escorts and preceded by a senior N.C.O. He was marched into the office and manoeuvred by the N.C.O., coming to a halt facing the Commanding Officer, seated at a table, whereupon the charge was read out and adjudicated on by the C.O. Now it so happened that the C.O. had a small vegetable plot outside his office. On this occasion the prisoner had been deemed guilty of a misdemeanour which obviously angered his adjudicator so much that he was about to deliver the severest reprimand possible. Having started his sentence "If this was my old regiment, I would have...", he suddenly stopped as we waited with bated breath for the finale. Looking out of the office window, he somewhat spoiled the dramatic denouement by turning to the warrant officer and proclaiming: "Brown, stop that dog from pissing on my peas!"

As a diverse group thrown together in the uncertain circumstances that prevailed during those early years of the war, characters inevitably emerged who would have a strong influence on sustaining our morale. "Pop" was one such person: the nickname was automatic as, like the C.O., he was of an age to have actually seen service in the Great War. This, coupled with his many years' experience in motor engineering, gained him the respect of us, his juniors, and the rapport between us all occasionally generated welcome humour at his expense. There were times when the younger instructors on the course would seek his views on certain engineering facts. Due to his long experience, and being capable of "flanneling", Pop would invariably reply that he was "not familiar with that type" [of equipment]. Eventually, much amusement would be caused by one of the younger members getting in first with: "You're not familiar with that type, Pop, are you?" But apart from his engineering skills, his forte was his talent as an excellent entertainer. Possessing a fine tenor voice, combined with the ability to accompany himself at the piano, he helped keep our spirits up when we were worried about the safety of distant homes and families. Whether it be in the N.A.A.F.I. aided by the ale at fourpence per pint in the evenings, or at weekends when we would invade the local pubs led by Pop, a good time would be guaranteed.

It was early autumn 1940 and we were now entering the final few weeks of our course. Having completed nearly three months' service, we had inevitably acquired some knowledge of how to manipulate the system. For this reason Ronnie and I were relaxing in the café on the top floor of the Woolworth's building overlooking Blackpool's Golden Mile, enjoying tea and toast instead of workshop activities back at the camp. We were good friends, with much in common, both having an interest in the London amateur boxing scene. Gazing out over the Irish Sea,

Ronnie suddenly turned to me and said: "Let's go home." Like me, I knew that he was worried about his family and the increasing enemy air activity in the South. So I instantly agreed to what was, in the circumstances, a far from sensible suggestion. Totting up our combined available finance, it was painfully obvious that our few bob would not get us very far by public transport, so the decision was taken to hitch-hike to London. Five minutes later, we were on our way, perched on the front seat of a milk float alongside the driver, who had readily agreed to allow us to accompany him to his depot on the edge of town.

Waiting on the trunk road for our next lift, we had no time to ponder our ludicrous position—having no pass, virtually no money and undertaking a round-trip of five hundred miles with the prospect of facing a charge of being Absent Without Leave—because the first heavy lorry we waved down stopped and we were on our way to Wigan. During the myriad journeys that I would experience through the following years, this one would remain etched in my memory. I experienced the all-pervasive spirit of togetherness and brotherhood that characterised those times. Quietly and without any acclaim, people were getting on with jobs despite having to endure extra burdens. This particularly applied to those three or four heavy goods vehicle drivers who willingly helped us to our eventual destination, even buying us food as they plied their way through the blackout. With their contemporaries, they were certainly unsung heroes of the war effort. With the blackout regulations of three thicknesses of tissue paper obscuring the side-lamps of their lorries and the two head-lamps fitted with hoods which subdued the beams almost to oblivion, they thundered their loads through the night, peering through windscreens three feet before them, at incredible speeds in the circumstances. They certainly put the "fear of God" into Ronnie and me, seated beside them. Although they carried what could be described as "loads for victory", they have been labelled by the uninitiated as "tramps on wheels". I'm sure that, like the London bus drivers who drove through the Blitz, they would have been plagued in later life by faulty eyesight, in addition to bad feet!

Our zig-zag journey southward through the various towns along the route, in those pre-motorway days, was prolonged for a spell as we were befriended by some ex-servicemen from the previous war. These amiable veterans, dressed in the uniform of a body grandly titled the Local Defence Volunteers (L.D.V.), were the forerunners of the Home Guard, later immortalised by the *Dad's Army* TV series. They insisted on supplying us with a great deal of ale to sustain us on our journey, interspersed with memories of their old campaigns. As a result of such a chequered journey, we did not arrive at Hammersmith Broadway until Saturday midday and, on parting, arranged to meet at midnight the following day, Sunday, at Euston Station, from where the last train to Blackpool departed.

As could be expected, my unannounced appearance on that Saturday afternoon was a source of great joy to my wife, family and everyone concerned, even though it was to be so short. There was the bonus, too, that my visit coincided with the fact my great friend Victor was also enjoying a 48-hour leave. He was well advanced into his aircrew training, which was denoted by the white flash in his forage cap and the three stripes on his arms. During celebrations we had much to discuss and I was delighted when he told me that he and Rosie, my wife's sister, planned to be married during his leave after he had completed his pilot training. I was to experience many weekend leaves in the years to come, but none of such short duration that produced so much happiness. On bidding a sad farewell on that Sunday evening, Dolly had placed a few pounds into my tunic pocket, so concerned was she that I should be able to buy a ticket back to Lancashire. It was to be a few years later that I learned she had "popped"—pawned—her ring to do so!

Ronnie and I met as arranged at Euston and boarded the midnight train to Blackpool along with hundreds of other servicemen, mostly airmen bound for the same destination as us. Throughout the war this train was the essential means of conveying them back to Blackpool and the neighbouring R.A.F. camps, to enable them to be present at the first working parades on Monday mornings. We both bought tickets but, while it was to be my fate to board this train many times in the future, it was the only time I could remember buying one! Rail tickets on training camps, certainly at Weeton during those years, were one of the most sought-after and important aspects of life. This was because for most of us, as trainees, the pay was negligible, free rail warrants scarce (four per year) and the distances needed to travel vast. Ticket evasion became essential, and the attempted alteration and forgery of old ticket dates became almost a cottage industry on the camp, similar to the production of cigarette lighters.

Likewise, various "scams", as they could be described, to avoid ticket collections on certain routes were learned and shared between airmen. This was aided by the scarcity of railway personnel, many of the younger employees themselves being in the Forces, leaving mostly a skeleton staff. One of these routes in particular was the journey from the local station, Kirkham and Wesham, to London and return, which could be travelled very cheaply once a 48-hour pass was obtained. No problem was experienced in boarding the London train at Kirkham; if necessary, a return ticket to the next stop, Preston, could be purchased. No tickets were collected or inspected on the train until it stopped just outside London, at Watford, where a number of ticket collectors boarded to collect all the tickets before it reached the terminus at Euston. But when the inspectors got on, those airmen with the Preston tickets got off, making their way to the electric rail platforms and travelling to their local station, where they proffered a fare from Watford with an appropriate excuse for the lack of a ticket.

Boarding that midnight train from Euston was not a problem for the "Erks" because they were able to bypass the ticket collector at the platform barrier—by simply gaining access to the platform and train via the entrance from the goods area! Again, no tickets were collected *en route* until leaving the train at Kirkham Station in the early hours of Monday morning. Here the final obstacle was generally an elderly porter to whom they would present the return half of their Preston ticket or, if they were without one, push past him, aided by the darkness, the width of the steep stone staircase and the sheer weight and volume of the "insurgents" pouring from the relatively narrow island platform.

On this occasion Ronnie and I, having experienced no actual travel problems, arrived back in camp with great trepidation about the form our reception would take and the possible consequences of our unauthorised absence. We need not have worried. Arriving at our hut and approaching our bed spaces, just as the lads were getting up and washing before breakfast, we found kitbags installed in our beds beneath the blankets in an effort to camouflage the fact that they were empty. We had also been "covered" in the technical area roll-calls by the same lads. Their actions were symbolic of the comradeship and togetherness of the times. These young men, as skilled tradesmen, would shortly be sent to theatres of war across the world. Many would be away from their loved ones and their homes for years, and some would never see them again. They should have been issued with the free railway warrants while it was still possible for them to visit their families, instead of having to resort to the less orthodox methods which we were forced to adopt.

As the course drew to an end, the time arrived for the trade tests to be taken. These were to be carried out by a small selection of technical N.C.O.s headed by the senior Flight Sergeant in charge of workshops. He was an ex-boy service regular and a popular character, known to the trainees by the nickname

"T.D.C.". This was an engineering term denoting "Top Dead Centre"—exactly the position in which he always wore his forage cap, which mostly crowned an impish grin. He was distinctly different from nearly everyone else, who tried to wear their caps at such an acute and jaunty angle that they almost appeared to be walking alongside them!

On the big day, we were assembled in the technical area while we waited to be individually called into the examiners' room for the tests, which were to be purely oral engineering questions. When I was called and as I passed the previous "Erk" making his exit from the room, he whispered helpfully to me: "If 'T.D.C.' asks how many drain plugs there are on a Crossley engine sump, there are two." (Crossley was the main heavy goods vehicle in use by the R.A.F. pre-war; every nut and bolt was known to the regular personnel.)

At the interview I confidently answered all the many questions that the panel threw at me, and was feeling quite pleased with myself until "T.D.C." asked me right at the end the question to which I had been alerted before my entrance. Glibly answering, as I had been advised, that there were of course two drain plugs, he then asked: "Why two?" Frankly, I did not know because I had not given it a thought so I was unable to reply immediately. As I left the room, "T.D.C." was wearing his impish grin as he explained quite simply that one plug was to drain the highest oil level and the other to drain the oil completely! A couple of days later, however, when the results appeared on the Personnel Occurrence Reports (P.O.R.s), I was surprised and delighted to find that I was among those who had been reclassified from Aircraftsman 2nd Class (A.C. 2) to Leading Aircraftsman (L.A.C.). Although I would be wearing henceforth a pair of propellers on the arms of my tunic, the real delight would be the much-needed increase in pay.

We would experience feelings of regret at having to end friendships due to postings and draftings during the coming years. But, as we parted from those with whom we had shared those first few months of shattering disruption to our young lives, we realised it was an era that we would never regret, or forget. This was particularly so on the evening of our farewell. The following morning we received a seven-day leave pass, accompanied this time by a free rail warrant, and the instructions that details of our next posting would be sent on to us later.

CHAPTER FOUR

The balloon goes up

BY THE autumn of 1940, the Blitz had begun to hit London devastatingly hard and the onslaught was to continue through the winter and into spring 1941. Between September 7 and November 13 1940, more than twelve thousand sorties were flown over the U.K. by the *Luftwaffe*. Over thirteen thousand tons of high explosive were dropped on London and almost a million incendiary bombs, in a relentless nightly offensive. A total of 13,000 people were killed in September and October alone, yet London's fortitude and resolve remained undimmed. Life continued to retain a semblance of normality as buses took commuters around shattered stations, ships continued to dock, and every morning people emerged blinking from their "rabbit holes" deep in the Tube, to inspect, with a mixture of phlegmatism and dismay, the latest wealds that had been lashed across the landscape overnight.

In fact, Goering never believed the Blitz would subdue Londoners' morale, and pleaded with Hitler to allow the bombers to attack small, more militarily important tactics, and he eventually got his way—beginning with the devastation of Coventry on the night of November 14/15.

But London still did not escape. The huge power station at Lots Road, on the banks of the Thames in Chelsea—in the shadows of whose four (German-built) chimneys I was brought up—supplied electricity for the capital's transport systems, and must have been a prime target for the *Luftwaffe* raiders. Just a quarter of a mile away, the Guinness Trust buildings had received a direct hit, with terrible consequences for their residents. Actual figures for deaths and other casualties were not available—nor were they sought—in those dark days.

In spring 1941, my wife and her family were living in Uverdale Road, which was even nearer the power station, so they and the other occupants of the houses and flats in the maze of little mean streets in the neighbourhood were having a hell-like time. It was during this period that I completed the training course at Weeton, and I was given my railway warrant to London. The journey south proved to be a nightmare after dark, with the train halted for long periods and mostly travelling at a snail's pace. At one time it actually crawled through the aftermath of an air attack, with burning buildings on each side of the tracks.

Reaching Euston in the early hours, it was just before dawn that I arrived on foot in Chelsea to the welcome sound of an all-clear siren. Only then did I learn that an unexploded landmine had settled on Uverdale Road and all the families, including my wife's, had been evacuated from the area. Eventually, after dawn, I discovered they had spent the night in St John's Mission Hall in the World's End. Fortunately, Dolly's brother was also on leave from the Army and we decided that in the few days we

47

had available, it was imperative that we improved the family's situation, particularly that of the young members. We had heard that newly-built houses were available for rent in the suburbs, where there was less danger from the raids. It did seem incomprehensible that it could be safer at the end of a Tube line just 15 miles away, but these were desperate times. On the same day, Joe and I had travelled down to South Ruislip on the Piccadilly Line and had found little difficulty arranging the monthly rental of one of the many new houses that were unoccupied.

Two days later, Joe and I, with a borrowed open lorry packed high with as much furniture (and family members) as the rather ancient vehicle could manage, ventured forth for a new—and, we hoped, safer—family home. I have often thought that the scene could have been reminiscent of Marie Lloyd's rousing music hall song *My old man said follow the van*! They were to spend the rest of the war in comparative safety in that house, although as it was next to the R.A.F.'s Northolt aerodrome, they experienced plenty of air raid activity. This airfield was the base from which a Polish fighter squadron operated successfully in the Battle of Britain in the pivotal summer and early autumn of 1940.

Even during the days of greatest danger, however, there were always incidents that were recalled later in a more light-hearted vein. One morning Dolly was shopping with her mother and the baby in the pram, alongside the airfield. Her mother remarked casually that a low-flying aircraft circling above had crosses on the wings. Immediately, volleys of machine gun fire burst from the aircraft as it started to strafe the fighters grounded on the airfield. Although the whole frightening incident lasted but a very short time, they both later recalled with amusement how they had tried to thrust their heads beneath the pram's hood to join the baby in an effort to escape injury.

It was during this leave that I was told my next posting would be to 954 Balloon Squadron and I was ordered to report to its headquarters in Weybridge, Surrey. On arrival, I was delighted to find that my friend Pop, the Great War veteran from the Weeton training course, was also there. While he was lodging in Weybridge, I was allocated a billet a few miles away in a large manor house at Byfleet, which was the base that controlled the balloon barrage surrounding the former Brooklands motor racing circuit and the Vickers aircraft factory. Before the balloon barrage had been installed around the complex, we were told, a *Luftwaffe* air raid had struck the factory just as the workers were changing shifts, with terrible consequences for lives and production. In accordance with the times, information was not broadcast but it was rumoured that a one-time foreign motor racing ace, who knew the track well, had led the attacking squadron that was responsible for the tragedy.

I was keen to make acquaintance with the race track, as before the war my uncle, Jack Wood, had raced there against such nationally known figures as Sir Malcolm Campbell, Kaye Don and Major Henry Segrave. Jack drove for the English Wolseley Car Company in addition to an Italian motor firm. As a young boy, I considered him a hero when I viewed his silver cups and particularly when I read newspaper accounts of him lapping Brooklands at the then amazing speed of 75mph!

I was astonished when I first saw the Brooklands track and the camouflage expertise that had been used to conceal it from the air. Holes had been drilled every few yards in the concrete to receive wooden poles of tree height, over which was netting interwoven with false foliage. There was, however, a space left between the poles under the netting in the centre of the track to allow narrow vehicles to travel around the perimeter; I was to take advantage of these on my R.A.F. Norton motorcycle combination at speed in an effort to emulate the feats of my uncle and his colleagues.

As the only transport mechanic on the base, my job was to service the machinery which allowed the balloons that formed the barrage to operate. There were eight balloon sites, spread equidistantly around the airfield, which were manned by crews who were designated balloon riggers and housed in the familiar R.A.F. huts. Although in a static position, each balloon was attached by 7,000ft of cable to a winch that was fitted on the rear chassis of a truck, which was powered by a Ford V8 engine. There was also a similar engine fitted next to the winch, which provided the power to pull the balloon down when required and allowed the cable to be wound on the winch drum. Maximum flying height of the balloons was 5,000ft, leaving always 2,000ft wound around the drum. I was soon to learn the importance of this engine being well-serviced because if it failed to start, and the balloon was unable to be lowered back to the winch, it would delay a crucial clearance report back to air control. The latter would need to know that the whole barrage was grounded at night to enable free passage for aircraft flying out low on missions.

At the time there were two or three smaller balloons that flew at a much lower height from manually-operated winches. These were specifically to combat dive-bombing. They had a large hand grenade device fitted to the cable at the winch base. The theory was that if a low-flying aircraft made contact with the cable, the grenade would catapult up and explode against the raiding aircraft. Also fitted to the cables of the main balloons when flying were two devices known as D.P.L.s (delayed parachute landings). One was fixed to the cable some height above the winch and the other a few feet below the balloon. Contact with the cable by an aircraft would activate the devices and the cable would be severed in two places, the balloon would be ripped and deflated, and two parachutes would descend, leaving the cable between—in theory—to wrap around the enemy aeroplane. It had been known for undue vibration on the cable when pulling down the balloon (such as by misuse of the clutch) to activate the devices, and the balloon with the cable to bid farewell to the winch! Imagine my apprehension, therefore, when I visited a site and observed a balloon operator astride the anchorage of the balloon's rigging, blissfully viewing the scenery from a hundred feet above the winch. It may have been boredom, or a bet—I didn't want to find out, that being a worry too far!

Barrage balloons may appear something of an antiquated oddity in today's world of smart bombs and sophisticated early-warning systems, but in both world wars they were one of the most important forms of anti-aircraft defence. Maintenance and operation of the balloons demanded skill, determination, mental alertness and much hard graft, and exposed the crews to the dangers of enemy aircraft and the hazards of the elements, from blizzards to lightning. It certainly was no "soft option" for the airmen who operated them.

The usual type of barrage balloon was a streamlined bag of rubber-proofed cotton fabric, specially treated, with a gas capacity of nearly 20,000 cubic feet, and about 63ft long and 31ft high. Weighing about 550lb, they were flown on a flexible steel cable and were filled with hydrogen, many times lighter than air. At the outbreak of war, as I discovered, they were flown directly from the leading-off gear at the back of their winches, all of which were motorised. The balloon crews originally consisted of two corporals and as many as ten men, but progress in balloon manipulation enabled it to be reduced to two corporals and eight men.

Balloons played a key tactical role in the battle against the *Luftwaffe*: they were not simply scarecrows, but were strategically distributed as part of the defensive "roof over Britain". By forcing enemy aircraft to fly higher than they wanted, they reduced the possibility of accurate bombing, and put the raiders into a position of the greatest vulnerability for attack by anti-aircraft guns and R.A.F. fighters.

Balloons and searchlights were positioned with great care, and some key factories were given the added protection of a P.A.C. (Parachute and Cable) installation. Similar to the D.P.L., it was typical of many Heath Robinsonian devices tested and occasionally used in wartime. It comprised a system of rockets which were fired electrically in the path of enemy aircraft. They were intended to carry light steel cables to a height of about 600ft, which were then lowered by parachute to enmesh enemy aircraft.

Barrage balloons soon established themselves, for civilians and service men and women alike, as a reassuring addition to the skyscape over Britain. The official War Office history of Britain's AA defences from 1939-42, *Roof Over Britain*, describes them piquantly as "at once logical and preposterous, comforting and extraordinary".

Although qualified mechanics, Pop and I were not initially familiar with winch mechanism so we were both sent on a course to the winch manufacturer at West Bromwich in the West Midlands. We were able to acquire the knowledge that we needed during the day, though the living conditions in the evening were rather grim. We were housed in a former mission hall which bore evidence of previous firebomb damage to its roof, and during our stay was certainly not immune to the nightly likelihood of further damage. However, Pop and I slept soundly through everything from the first evening. We had found a local pub with a piano in its lounge. The landlord soon recognised that Pop's prowess on the keys, combined with our repertoire of songs, increased the sale of his ale, and he showed his appreciation by not charging for the beer we both drank. Further, his customers, mostly civilians employed in a large munitions factory, would be generous when, at the end of the evening's revelries, he would organise a collection on our behalf. At the end of the course we returned to our base fortified with not only the necessary technical knowledge but also some memories that would remain with us for decades to come.

If you were involved with Training Command, it inevitably meant you would have to endure constant contact with hundreds of personnel at the large training camps. Although this would not appeal to most people if given the choice, it could have its advantages: the more people you encountered, the greater was the possibility of making contact with someone whose intellect and wisdom would leave an indelible impression on your memory. Although I was eventually destined to be attached to Training Command for a long period, I could count such experiences on one hand. But I consider myself very fortunate in having made such an acquaintance while stationed at that small balloon unit in Byfleet.

Space in the manor house where we were billeted was allocated, of course, according to rank. Our one junior officer was installed in a large room on the second floor of the building, which had an *en suite* bathroom, while all the others shared rooms and bed space according to rank; I shared a bedroom with a corporal and most rooms had two or three beds. There was a large communal games room on the ground floor so the building could be considered, in the circumstances, a comfortable billet. Above the third floor, in the roof, however, was an attic in which there was a small room just big enough for one bed. This was allocated to the lowest rank in the R.A.F., an Aircraftsman Second Class, a Scot, predictably known as "Jock", whose duties were solely to maintain the cleanliness of the building. Despite these menial responsibilities, I was to consider myself privileged to have known him and was proud to have had an opportunity to form a firm friendship with him. Initially I recognised him as a fellow socialist but I soon became aware of the wide knowledge he possessed about political and religious matters in general; in fact, his entire scholarship was very superior to my own.

True to form, he loved his whisky, although frequently he loved it too unreservedly, which manifested itself at times by the strain on his and my exchequer. If any programme of a vaguely cerebral nature was being broadcast on his small radio, I would join him in his attic room. We sometimes listened to the popular Professor Joad series, and in the pub later, the more he imbibed, the greater he would expound his own views on the topic of the professor's lecture. He was a devotee of Robbie Burns, of whose work he had an immense knowledge, and, like his fellow Scot, he had a great wit and, when in his cups, also a roving eye. I can recall an occasion when, as a very attractive young woman left the bar-room, he told me that he had seduced her. Seeing my look of utter disbelief, he added: "Wi' my eyes, lad, wi' my eyes."

I was interested in his background and learned that before joining the R.A.F. he had been a cinema manager in London. But he had formerly been a waiter in an exclusive restaurant in the centre of the capital, whose clientele was largely made up of those who were "something in the City". Once, while serving lunch to a table of such types who were engaged in an animated discussion about a political issue, one diner patronisingly asked: "What's Jock's opinion?" Apparently the answer they received was so profound and erudite that it became a habit for them and other diners to invite "Jock, the waiter's" views on subjects that would benefit from an intellectual input. This eventually was even featured in the local press and became an innovation that proved a promotional asset to the restaurant—and also, of course, to "Jock, the waiter". I could never reconcile myself to the fact that a man of such intellect and learning should be sub-servient to a senior N.C.O. whose ignorance was such that he continually took a delight in berating my friend for his cleaning skills, and—as a prelude to his criticisms—referring to him al-ways as "Haggis". Of course, this is another consequence of war: not only its physical destruction and the visible carnage but also its devaluing of learning and education, as it eradicates opportu-nity, hope and prospects of progress.

During my service with the balloon squadron, sadly, I cannot report any successes with regard to destruction of enemy aircraft. However, there were few dull moments, and on some days life could even be described as hectic. This was particularly the case when a freak flash of lightning simultaneously struck three cables, bringing the three balloons blazing to the ground and distributing three separate 5,000ft lengths of cable across the countryside. This cable ended up strewn across railway tracks, and entwined around chimney stacks and even a church steeple, and had to be retrieved as soon as possible or, according to orders received, even sooner. This in itself proved no mean job. In addition, three separate 7,000ft lengths of cable had to be rewound to each winch and three new balloons inflated with gas and re-rigged. Meanwhile, the control room awaited the completion of all this work to enable it to report to air control that the balloon barrage was indeed compete and flying, after twenty-four hours of continuous hard work.

Service during wartime is always in a state of flux and transition, so my stay at 954 Balloon Squadron proved to last less than three months. Having received information that places on a new course for Group One fitters were available back at Weeton, I applicd and was quickly accepted. While I would greatly miss my friends at Byfleet, the opportunity to re-muster to the top skilled group, with the resulting pay rise, was, I calculated, essential to my family's finances.

CHAPTER FIVE

Welcome back to Weeton

MANY CHANGES had taken place by the time I arrived back at Weeton No. 8 School of Technical Training to join the first entry on a new transport fitters' course later in spring 1941. The last time I was there, the previous year, I had witnessed the weary remnants of part of the Polish Air Force arriving from goodness knows where, still dressed in long black coats, leather belts and berets; now they were fully kitted out in R.A.F. uniforms, with new equipment, and were installed in their own Wing. In addition, a new Wing had been created to accommodate the many recruits to the Women's Auxiliary Air Force (W.A.A.F.s) who were to join training courses for trades, one of which was motor mechanic.

Changes, meanwhile, had also been taking place 250 miles to the south, in London, where the British Union of Fascists' leader Oswald Mosley had been interned in May 1940.[1] In 1941, however, in the somewhat less salubrious living conditions we were experiencing in north Lancashire, it was a very gloomy period of the war and generally the news about any progress made by our troops and their allies did not lend itself to celebration. Most worrying of all was that the enemy air attacks on our major cities and ports were increasing, with the resulting destruction. Although our camp was not subjected to these raids, there was probably no-one at Weeton who was free from the constant anxiety about their families and loved ones who were not so fortunate. After just a couple of weeks of my course, I was to be sent the most shattering news I had ever received. I had been expecting an announcement about the date of my friend Victor's marriage to my wife's sister, due at any time on the completion of his pilot training course. But the message I eventually received from Dolly was a heart-rending rather than celebratory one: on Victor's final passing-out flight, his aircraft had crashed, killing him and a co-pilot.

In a state of shock and gripped by a feeling of helplessness and hopelessness, I could only think of getting home. It was midweek and I went to see "Poff" in the squadron office, a great N.C.O. and a friend to anyone in need. I put my case to be considered for compassionate leave and, although he was sympathetic, he was very doubtful as there were so many applications at that time. But he was eventually able to secure for me a twenty-four-hour pass and rail warrant for that weekend, for which I was enormously grateful. The initial shock was soon replaced by a deep sadness but also by a great anger. Why, I thought, should that handsome boy, just out of his teens and possessed of such fine mental and physical attributes, combined with a genuinely kind nature, be sacrificed—and for what? In retrospect I realised that I had never thought of him as a fighter pilot. Yes, he had the necessary education and physical qualifications but he had never even driven a car! Was he another service example of square pegs in round holes?

In my grief, my mind was stumbling around for someone or something to blame. I remembered him as my dear pre-war friend. His aspirations, his love of music and of the girl he was determined to make his bride, living a life eventually in that "house on the hill" about which he sang so beautifully and plaintively—all these were now so brutally obliterated. This was evil and unnecessary, I thought. If the latter, then why had I volunteered? Well, to fight against fascism. Did such a cause therefore make a war just? In the turmoil of my thoughts, I was not to realise how much more there was to come.

My weekend's compassionate leave could only be filled with grief and mourning, as it proved, accentuated by the interminable raids of the *Luftwaffe*. These raids brought home to me the stark fact that my young son was in his second year and had never spent a night in the comfort of a bedroom, always in an air raid shelter. On my return to camp, I successfully applied for a sleeping out pass (S.O.P.) which was to enable my wife and him to have at least a few weeks' respite from the inhuman suffering that always befalls civilian families during wartime. But, of course, securing a room in bustling Blackpool for a few weeks in those wartime days was not without its difficulties and, once obtained, it was not exactly an idyllic existence; nevertheless, in the circumstances, it proved very therapeutic for them both.

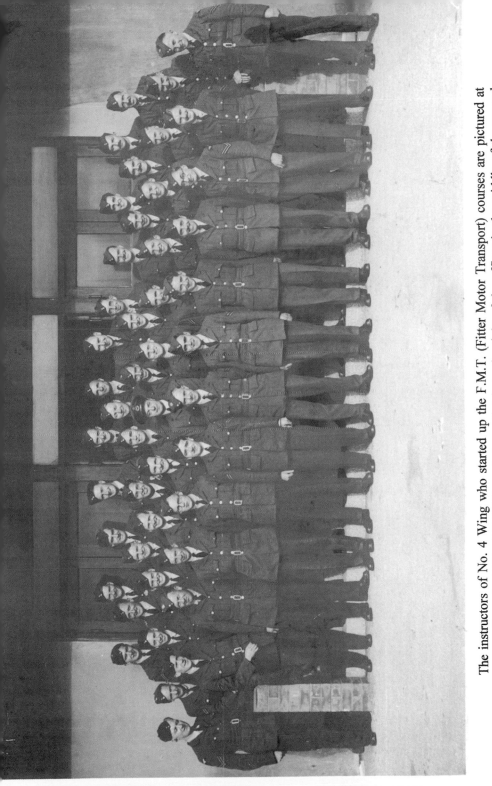

The instructors of No. 4 Wing who started up the F.M.T. (Fitter Motor Transport) courses are pictured at Weeton Camp in 1941. Alf Goldberg is immediately to the right of the officer in the middle of the second row, in the centre of the photograph, and his friend Arthur is behind and to the left of the officer.

Concrete anti-invasion blocks are strung along the promenade in this 1940s view of Blackpool's Golden Mile and Central Pier, packed with visitors and vehicles.

Blackpool's baroque ballrooms were a "league of nations" for service people from all over the world during the war. Here, crowds pack the balconies and line the dance floor of the exquisitely decorated Tower Ballroom as the organist plays the "mighty Wurlitzer".

The author with an entry of West African trainees at the W.A.A.C. station at Takoradi in 1944.

West African paradise … palm trees, crystal-clear waters and golden sands were among the fringe benefits of life in Takoradi.

Alf Goldberg resplendent, though no doubt perspiring, in the ceremonial robes of the local tribal chief in which, at the invitation of the trainees, he was photographed before returning home from the Gold Coast.

The officers and N.C.O.s in charge of the courses at Takoradi W.A.A.C. camp in 1944. Alf Goldberg is standing at the end of the back row on the right and the Squadron Leader and Commanding Officer is second left on the front row.

Later, during a leave, I returned with them to Dolly's family in the London suburb where, despite no lessening of the uncertainties of their lives, there was no sense of despair, only one of endurance, determination and comradeship. During this leave Dolly had even succeeded in being enrolled on a training course as a welder by a local engineering firm, in preparation for work on Army tanks. This was made possible by her being able to place our son in a Government-subsidised nursery for the princely sum of one shilling a day, including all meals, which was open for fifteen hours from six in the morning. This illustrated what could be achieved by a Government in war, even though most administrations did not consider such child care a necessity in peacetime!

Back at Weeton, many new trade courses were starting, resulting in hundreds more personnel—men and women—passing through the camp. I had successfully completed my own course and it was then with some foreboding that I learned that I would be retained on the course as an instructor. Although two stripes and another pay rise were gratefully accepted, life on a Training Command camp, with all its regulations, was not to be so welcome.

The year 1941 was a very grim one in all aspects of the war; even the winter weather turned out to be diabolical, with the camp becoming almost snowbound—unusually for the Fylde Coast, as its low-lying nature and closeness to the sea meant snow was rarely a problem. The coal distribution vehicles were unable to operate around the camp, so personnel had to visit the main coal yard to fill sacks and then drag them back to their huts. This must have been a hard initiation for the newly arrived W.A.A.F.s spending their first winter away from home. For me and most of my socialist-minded friends, however, halfway through that very dark and gloomy year something very important happened which greatly lifted our spirits. This was the news in June that Hitler had broken his non-aggression pact with Stalin and his army had attacked the Soviet Union. We knew that he had this time made a great mistake and misjudgement in attacking that vast country, with its cruel climate and often bleak and inhospitable landscape. We also knew about the endurance and resilience of its people. Perhaps we did have an inflated view of the Russians' prowess and capabilities, and we were of course unaware at the time of the brutality of Stalin's regime, but time was to prove our judgement correct.

During that year, the camp's boundaries continued to expand as more trade courses were introduced and, as the personnel grew in numbers, so did the discipline tighten. More working parades and church parades, along with guard and fire duties, did not contibute towards making a happy camp in those dismal days. Yet life remained rich in emotion, warmth, friendship, and at times, of course, pathos. Amid the seething activity, natural humour abounded. One Sunday, for example, when a senior N.C.O. had shepherded the last few lads in through the doors for church parade, I heard the stentorian command: "Take your hat off in the house of God—you stupid bastard!" (Incidentally, as I am Jewish, I am not sure why I was there in the first place; perhaps it was because the forces at that time seemed unable to pigeon-hole anyone who wasn't Church of England, Roman Catholic or Methodist.)

On another occasion, when I was in a squadron office at Weeton Camp, a young trainee entered and asked for a form to apply for a commission. His request unfortunately happened to be made to a life-serving Warrant Officer, who was so ignorant that, according to the trainees on his Wing, even the other W.O.s noticed it! Clearly incensed, he demanded of the trainee: "And what makes you think that you have the qualities to become an officer in the R.A.F.?" Whereupon the now-nervous applicant started to relate how he had passed his matriculation examination at school and later been accepted for a place at university before being called up for service. At that point he was abruptly interrupted by the N.C.O. declaring loudly: "Never mind about all this bullshit. Have you got your school leaving certificate?"!

The squadron office was the scene of another bizarre encounter which I witnessed, when an "Erk" wandered in one day and requested an application form for an extension of service. Asked by the clerk about the number of extra years he wanted to serve, he replied: "Three." Then the clerk told him he was a "bloody nuisance" as he only had forms for a seven-year period, and the "Erk" would have to wait while he went to another room to obtain the necessary paperwork. The lad replied: "Don't bother—the seven-years form will do." How could he, I thought, sacrifice four years of his life ... just to stop a guy having to go next door!

NOTE

[1] As I wrote in volume one of these memoirs, although we never met, Mosley's life and mine sometimes seemed inextricably interlaced. Indeed, from 1940 we both found ourselves in institutions that demanded tight discipline (though the regime at Weeton was probably more rigorous than the one he enjoyed in Holloway Prison).

The outbreak of war was to face British fascism with a crisis of conscience that would eventually bring it to its knees. Mosley's line was that he would do nothing to sabotage the war effort but would seek to overthrow the Government democratically and work for a negotiated peace. However, the B.U.F. received a derisory share of the vote in the handful of parliamentary by-elections it contested in 1940. On May 22 Parliament rushed through amendments to the Defence Regulations, which empowered the Home Secretary, John Anderson, to imprison without trial anyone he believed was likely to be a threat to the safety of the nation. Early the following day, Mosley was arrested at his flat in Dolphin Square and taken to Brixton Prison, where he was held with other fascist detainees in 'F' wing. (In this case, the word 'wing' indicated something slightly different from its meaning for my R.A.F. camp at Weeton!) In 1942 Herbert Morrison, who had succeeded Anderson as Home Secretary, made arrangements to allow detained husbands and wives to live together. The Mosleys had a four-roomed house within the grounds of Holloway Prison with facilities to cook their own meals and permission to pay other detainees to perform domestic services. It seemed that class divisions transcended even considerations of national security and penal policy!

Naturally, we anti-fascists were unhappy at the kid-glove treatment which we thought was being accorded to the B.U.F. leader and his wife, Lady Diana

Mosley (who died in summer 2003 aged 93, as this book was being produced). This disenchantment was heightened in November 1943 when Morrison released the couple on doctor's evidence that Oswald Mosley was suffering from thrombo-phlebitis, and that continued imprisonment might permanently endanger his health or even kill him. As part of the terms of his release, Mosley had to report monthly to the police, take part in no political activities and, without police permission, was to travel no more than seven miles from his home in Oxfordshire. These restrictions were to remain in force until V.E. Day, May 8 1945. Labour MPs reacted furiously to his release and in Downing Street an angry crowd of war workers called for the decision to be reversed. It was not to be, but Mosley—and British fascism—were effectively finished as a serious political force.

A former Labour Cabinet minister who had seemed destined for a meteoric political career, Sir Oswald Ernald Mosley was a dashing but deeply flawed minor aristocrat who had set up his ill-fated New Party in 1931 and the following year formed the B.U.F. In October 1936 I was present at the infamous 'Battle of Cable Street' when the B.U.F. 'Blackshirts' clashed with police and anti-fascist demonstrators in the East End. Although I was there in little more than an observer's capacity—on the periphery of a crowd later estimated at some 100,000—I am proud to be able to say I witnessed this historic confrontation that was to mark the start of British fascism's decline.

Closer to home, however, I had experienced the Blackshirts' antics three years earlier when the B.U.F. took over the former Whitelands teacher training college in the King's Road, Chelsea, as their HQ. The building, known as the "Black House", was only a stone's throw from my home on the first floor of terraced block in Dartrey Road in the neighbouring World's End area. At that time, as now, the Royal Borough of Chelsea was characterised by appalling extremes of wealth and poverty, the brash affluence of the King's Road contrasting with the deprivation of the World's End. Bizarrely, the block which we shared with five other families was named Westmorland House, after an English county that was world's away from the dankness of the World's End, both geographically and aesthetically. Yet, despite the conditions, there was an indomitable solidarity among the people who lived there, and it was these bonds of brotherhood that enabled us to put up such fierce resistance to the fascists when they moved in as our near-neighbours. Working as a motor mechanic at Moon's garage on the edge of the West End, I was able to observe the fascists' activities at first hand as some of Mosley's vehicles were stabled with us. Occasionally I would watch as he arrived at the garage to be driven away in one of his limousines to Croydon Airport; sometimes the party would return later with a "V.I.P" who was pretty obviously a high-ranking official from Nazi Germany.

These were febrile times, marked by economic and political uncertainty, and they were just the sort of conditions that provided a fertile breeding ground for the fledgling fascist movement, uniting disaffected right-wing members of the upper classes and misguided working class people in a horrifying hybrid. Café society met the mean streets in a potentially explosive cocktail. And it was particularly disturbing for a young man of Jewish background such as myself: my grandparents had escaped the Russian pogroms at the turn of the 20th century, and—though Mosley initially tended to play it down—it was clear that anti-Semitism would form a major plank of the B.U.F.'s policy platform, particularly with such a large Jewish community settled on the other side of the city in the East End.

The Black House became the fulcrum of fascism in Britain, the centre of a whirl of extreme-right activity that seemed to grow ever more aggressively and overtly racist. As we walked past the building near the Duke of York's Territorial Army HQ on our way towards Sloane Square and the city centre, we would watch with appalled fascination as the processions of armour-plated cars and black-uniformed fascists entered and left the substantial building. The Black House—which was its official name, though we referred to it as the "Fascist Fort"—had lecture rooms, dormitories, a gymnasium and a parade ground, and, in an emergency, the B.U.F. claimed 5,000 Blackshirts could live there as a self-contained unit. According to the B.U.F. propagandists, it reverberated to the sound of laughter, song and manly conversation, but the reality was to be found in the cellars beneath. There, the Blackshirts had prepared the cells for the day when they could seize political opponents and bring them in for punishment, as the Stormtroopers had done in Hitler's "Brown Houses". One even had a skull and crossbones on the door and was known as the "death cell". It's also not beyond the realms of speculation that these cells were sometimes used to house members of the B.U.F. themselves. The Blackshirts, many recruited from the terminally disenchanted, were an unruly bunch and, rather than have these disciplinary lapses exposed to the police and public, their leaders often preferred a rough and ready form of "in-house" punishment. By 1935, however, they had quit the Black House, much to the relief of me and my fellow anti-fascists in the World's End.

CHAPTER SIX

Accidental heroes in Blackpool

AUTUMN 1942 saw me still instructing, along with my friend Arthur, who had travelled the identical path with me since we had met, initially as civilians, on the train to R.A.F. Cardington. Although we had both reached the lofty rank of sergeant and were experiencing the comparative comforts of the sergeants' mess, we knew that we had to get away from Training Command. We had spent well over a year mostly in classrooms instructing new recruits on engine and transmission theory. As this involved more than fifty new entrants each week, it became very demanding and we had to adopt a case-hardened attitude. While most trainees were willing and co-operative, there were always members of the "awkward squad" to deal with. In addition, during that year, R.A.F. Command had discovered from some source that personnel engaged on technical duties were supposedly inefficient in armed combat. Therefore, everyone involved in instructional duties would be required to include armed combat in their schedules. After a crash course in those skills, I found myself instructing my trainees for one half-day a week in, of all things, the art of bayonet-fighting!

At this time Arthur and I were volunteering for every advertised transfer, without any success, until one afternoon in October, while at work, I received a notification that read simply: "Senior N.C.O.s needed to volunteer for a special job in a hot climate." I contacted Arthur at work and we both decided to put our names forward, as usual. Within a couple of hours, we received instructions to report to the medical centre at once. Baffled, we duly reported, to learn that they had instructions from the posting and drafting centre on the camp that we were both to be given a number of specified injections immediately. We replied that we wanted to know more about these sudden developments before we agreed to any medical treatment, so we walked across to the posting and drafting centre. There, we were told that they knew nothing more than what was in the instructions from above, and that the job we had volunteered for was urgent. Further instructions about posting arrangements would be notified shortly.

Perturbed by the suddenness of these arrangements, in contrast to the normally slow-rumbling mechanism of the military bureaucracy, we decided that we would have to succumb to the medical treatment. Revisiting the medical centre, we were given the injections, except one for yellow fever that we were told was not available and would be administered later, which certainly did not increase our confidence in what was happening. By now, the speed of events, combined with the effect of the injections, was making us both feel somewhat resentful. We agreed that there was no way in which we going to travel perhaps halfway across the world without first seeing our families.

As senior N.C.O.s, we were able to request a meeting with an officer so, deciding that the situation was urgent and warranted immediate action, we visited the headquarters unit, where we sought an interview with the Commanding Officer. We were surprised to be ushered into the Group Captain's presence quite quickly, but even more surprised by the reception we received. He knew of the circumstances and explained how pleased he was that two of his senior N.C.O.s had so promptly volunteered for this special job, which had come from high in the Air Ministry and of which even he had no detailed knowledge. By now I was a little apprehensive and I knew that Arthur would be feeling likewise because, after all, we only wanted to get away from the camp and not engage in anything approaching heroics! Eventually, when we managed to raise the subject of leave, he was sympathetic and explained that he understood this affair was most urgent and so any time for a leave period in the circumstances would hardly be possible. After listening to our respective stories of woe, however, he intimated that if we gave him our solemn word to return to camp immediately we received a telegram to do so, he would sanction a leave pass. We readily agreed to his offer and gave him our profuse thanks and a smart salute before leaving.

Our next visit was to the Wing office where, filling in the pass forms, we decided to apply for a period of ten days before presenting them to the Warrant Officer for signing. In view of the length of leave time we requested, the W.O. contacted the head-quarters unit for verification, and received the reply that length of leave was immaterial as we would probably be recalled within forty-eight hours!

Next morning found us both on the Blackpool train heading for home; he for Canterbury, me for London. Because of the circumstances, this leave was always going to be a sad and emotional one, and so it proved. As we expected it would be very brief, farewells were being said almost from the start. Coupled with the fact that the nightly air raids were extremely regular and persistent, it did not lend itself to anything approaching a tranquil and restful spell of leave. Most surprising, however, was the fact that at the end of the ten days' allotted period, I still had not been recalled. Though this was a very welcome bonus, it did not lessen the grief of the final parting from the family for a long and perhaps unknown period. I met Arthur at Euston Station and, in a sombre mood, we boarded the familiar midnight train bound for Blackpool and our journey back to Weeton Camp. Reporting to the posting and drafting centre at the camp, however, we were astonished to learn that they had received no further information whatever about our posting. As we had been officially cleared from the staff, we agreed to report every morning to the centre pending further instructions. As far as we were concerned, this was an admirable arrangement as it enabled us still to live on camp but to visit the attractions of nearby Blackpool at our will. Then, on the third morning of reporting, we were informed that our instructions had been received. We had been posted to, of all places ... Blackpool.

Blackpool will need little explanation for most people. Perched precariously on the tip of the rectangular Fylde peninsula, on the windswept Irish Sea coast of north-west Lancashire, Blackpool was a product of the entrepreneurialism and industrialisation of the Victorian era, virtually pioneering the phenomenon of mass tourism.

Formerly a tiny coastal settlement, with just a huddle of houses and hotels at the end of the eighteenth century, it was transformed by an economic and social revolution into Europe's first and most popular working-class holiday resort, in its heyday attracting some seventeen million visitors a year. While rival re-sorts briefly prospered from middle-class visitors seeking to "take the waters", as was fashionable at the time, Blackpool soon abandoned all pretensions to gentility and carved out a unique niche as the workingman's watering place. The 'Wakes Week' holidays in the North, with entire textile towns shutting down and their population decamping *en bloc* to the seaside, provided a continuous source of business for the resort during a holiday season that was lengthened by the two months of the Illumina-tions—the "Greatest Free Show on Earth".

Modelled on Monsieur Eiffel's in Paris, Blackpool's 518ft 9in Tower, opened in 1894 though only half the height of its French rival, has brooded over the surrounding flatlands of the Fylde Coast for more than a century. Even in its truncated wartime form when its topmost section was lopped off and it was temporarily rigged up as an emergency radar station, the Tower remained a commanding presence ... not to mention a handy landmark for aircraft, both friendly and hostile. Meanwhile, Blackpool's three piers strode boldly out into the Irish Sea as a reminder of the days when a stroll along their wooden boardwalks was the nearest many people could get to a sea voyage. The oldest, the little-changed North Pier, opened as early as 1863. It would be unfair (though probably accurate) to say that the town prospered from the war, but thanks to its role as a military training centre, the mystique of the Golden Mile soon became embedded in the consciousness (for good or ill) of hundreds of thousands of service personnel, many of whom returned on honeymoon in the marriage boom that followed the conflict.

Blackpool was the antithesis of any other British town at war. Entertainment flourished as in peacetime, and its leisure industry catered for an international army of service personnel to assure its ascendancy. Frequently, during the winter, the many bar counters of the Tower, Winter Gardens and Palace ballrooms were thronged three-deep with what could be described as a "League of Nations", from all corners of the world, anxious to be served. In the summer, the famous Golden Mile was thronged with visitors as Blackpool became a cosmopolitan melting pot, bringing together a cocktail of cultures, with Poles and Americans, Dutch and French, Scandinavians and Canadians mingling along the promenade or in the great baroque ballrooms. Their uniforms made a kaleidoscopic combination of colours and there was a barely credible buoyancy about Blackpool as Hitler's hordes stormed west across Europe. A 1941 souvenir programme for the Blackpool Tower and Winter Gardens ("War price 4d") remarked with laconic stoicism: "In the event of an air raid warning being received during a performance, the audience will be informed at once from the stage. It should be remembered that the warning does not necessarily mean that a raid will take place and that in any case it is not likely to occur for at least five minutes. Anyone who desires to leave the theatre may do so, but the performance will continue and members are advised in their own interests to remain in the building."

Yet to me the town always remained a mass of inconsistencies, with the prosperous entertainment scene but a veneer for the hardship, heartache and pathos beneath. Many of the service personnel, making the most of the entertainment, were awaiting drafting and posting to theatres of war across the world. Their experiences in Blackpool were a final, defiant, valediction before they attuned themselves once more to the realities of war, thousands of miles from home. (Today the resort is still a bundle of contradictions, though for different reasons: the Golden Mile may have lost its seedy charm, but the neon glitz and glamour of the seafront conceal a hinterland of bedsits and sub-standard accommodation that puts the town near the top of the national league table for urban poverty and deprivation.)

Many people from diverse nations formed part of the community of Blackpool during those dark days. Early in the war, the Blitz on the London docks caused great damage and destruction to the East End, resulting in many of its residents seeking refuge in the comparative safety of the Lancashire resort. In fact, some of the cafés and tea rooms along the promenade (where visitors often had to run the gauntlet of kerbside traders, hucksters and black-marketeers selling watches and jewellery) were reminiscent to me of Mile End Road or Aldgate.

One character who took part in that exodus was known around the East End as "Flash Harry" because he always visited the markets, immaculately dressed, driving a limousine. He had been driving an A.R.P. car during an air raid when a near-miss blew a wheel off the vehicle, so on his recovery he sought safer climes for his wife and himself. He advertised himself as "Uncle Harry" and worked on the Golden Mile, at that time a somewhat ramshackle *demi-monde* of the weird and the wonderful, combining stalls and "freak shows", which was a haven for him and his unorthodox talents. He was a showman in the true sense of the word, able to gather a crowd around him with ease, and this ability proved lucrative for him and those who would hire him for that purpose on the Golden Mile. I knew him well and, when I was able, I would get a lot of pleasure in watching him at work, manipulating and entertaining a crowd. I also knew that the great comedian Max Miller had also been an admirer before the war, in London, insisting that Harry was photographed with him as a form of appreciation.

It was due to Harry that I unexpectedly gained an insight into the existence of a very small and little-noticed—yet extraordinary—part of the community of Blackpool. During 1941 when I had just been made an N.C.O., he directed me towards a few people he said he wanted me to meet. They consisted of six or seven women and a few children, standing in a group on the edge of a crowd he had been addressing on the seafront. By way of introduction, he asked me to tell them my name, which I did, although I considered the request rather odd. I was immediately surprised at the reaction this produced from them as they all seemed to stare at me in disbelief, and one woman exclaimed: "But you can't be Jewish!" I looked quizzically at Harry, who quickly explained that they could not believe that someone with my name could even be allowed in the R.A.F., never mind serve as an N.C.O. After we had chatted some more, it emerged that these women and children were part of a group that had successfully been smuggled out of occupied Europe and eventually brought to Blackpool to recuperate. Meeting them served as a lesson to me, as it was my first real understanding of the deep suffering that had befallen the victims of those occupied territories, because even in comparative safety, the horrors they had survived were still with them, particularly in their eyes.

From the beginning of the war, Blackpool had lent itself perfectly to the R.A.F. as a centre for training operations. First, and most importantly, it was on the far west coast, largely out of the line of enemy fire, and therefore training was unlikely to be interrupted by air raids.

Secondly, it had the accommodation that was so vitally needed: tens of thousands of beds in its many hotels and boarding houses. Next, it had unrivalled transport links for a provincial town, with no fewer than three railway lines converging on the resort. And, finally, it had the room for troop training: the sandy beaches and wide promenade became impromptu parade grounds, and were ideal sites for exercises and square-bashing, while huge buildings like the Victorian Winter Gardens complex, now Grade 2* listed, could comfortably house indoor activities such as Morse code training and pay parades. The Morse sessions took place in the vast Olympia building, and troops marching by had to break step to avoid disrupting the lessons. Gymnastic exercises were staged on the 12,500-square foot sprung floor of the barrel-vaulted, gilt-decorated Empress Ballroom, the work of the famous designer Frank Matcham, who was also responsible for the sumptuous Grand Theatre, which had opened in the same year as the Tower. In 1934 the ballroom was re-floored with 10,000 pieces of oak, walnut, mahogany and greenwood, laid on 1,320 four-inch springs. During the Great War the ballroom had been requisitioned by the Admiralty to assemble gas envelopes for airships. As far as the more mundane matter of sleeping accommodation was concerned, the Government estimated Blackpool's hotels and boarding houses could comfortably absorb an extra 109,000 permanent residents, which would virtually double the size of its resident population.

At the time, R.A.F. Station Blackpool, which was officially opened a month after the outbreak of war, was said to be the biggest military training installation in the world. This is impossible to prove, but a staggering total of more than three-quarters of a million recruits received their basic training there, and at peak times there were 45,000 airmen in the town, spread across 5,000 lodging houses. To this day R.A.F. Blackpool is remembered with a mixture of fondness and frustration by former wartime airmen and National Servicemen the length and breadth of Britain.

Many landladies, struggling to make ends meet after the declaration of war and the attenuation of the 1939 season, were able to recoup their losses by accommodating R.A.F. personnel. Indeed, the war was to have a major impact on the legendary Blackpool landlady, the butt of so many end-of-the-pier jokes. Despite—or perhaps because of—the hostilities, Blackpool enjoyed something of a property boom in the early 1940s. Many inexperienced newcomers were attracted by the prospect of making easy money in the resort's hotel industry, and if they needed a second income they could supplement their hotel earnings by munitions or other war work. The war also spawned the phenomenon of the "pirate" landladies. The demands of billeting tens of thousands of service people in Blackpool put huge pressure on the established hotels and boarding houses, so, with entrepreneurial flair typical of the resort, some private householders in non-holiday areas went into the accommodation business. These unofficial billets provided a useful source of tax-free income for their owners.

Like any other army, the battalions of hotel landladies marched on their stomachs, and with characteristic resourcefulness and stoicism the landlady soon adjusted herelf to rationing. She would simply collect together her visitors' ration books and buy the necessary produce from her usual local suppliers, whose stocks would have been increased accordingly. And, of course, some of them contrived ways of circumventing the wartime food shortages: one particularly ingenious landlady even reportedly provided fresh salmon regularly for high tea on Sundays.

The war also had an unexpected knock-on effect on the town's flourishing football club, which at that time was a major force in the old First Division. The club's success in the post-war era—including three F.A. Cup Final appearances in five years, climaxing in the famous victory of 1953—has been partly attributed to the town's proximity to R.A.F. bases. Many former professionals serving in the R.A.F. played as "guests" for the club, and Blackpool were one of the top footballing sides in the makeshift leagues that functioned during the war; some of the players stayed on at Bloomfield Road when hostilities ended.

But R.A.F. Blackpool was also the hub of a much wider concentration of air bases—mine at Weeton, Kirkham (now a "Category D" open prison), Inskip (subsequently HMS Inskip, a Royal Navy listening post, with its eerie radio masts still looming over the flat landscape of the Fylde plain), and the huge American U.S.A.A.F. complex at Warton, known as B.A.D. (Base Air Depot) 2. At its peak, some 10,000 American airmen were stationed at B.A.D. 2. The entry of the USA into the war in 1941 had brought further ethnic diversity to the Fylde, particularly their black airmen, as well as the awesome spending power of the dollar. Today the site retains its aviation links as a major British Aerospace plant (now BAe Systems) producing among others the new Eurofighter, known as the Typhoon. Airmen from Warton, and its sister base at Burtonwood near Warrington, would pour into Blackpool in the evenings and at weekends, turning the town into a seething whirlpool of different accents and uniforms—flat Lancastrian vowels mixing with Texan drawls as locals rubbed shoulders with these exotic visitors from across the Atlantic.

Meanwhile, thousands of British troops were whisked daily by a fleet of trams to the rifle ranges at Rossall, near Fleetwood, where extra sidings and a loop line were laid by the corporation tramways department in autumn 1940 to accommodate the additional traffic, which included ammunition. A section of the tram works in Rigby Road, Blackpool, became an R.A.F. wireless school while the stores were used as a N.A.A.F.I. The trams themselves—some now driven by women—were painted in an all-over green wartime livery with their headlights shielded by hoods. Special covers even had to be fitted to parts of the overhead wire catenary on the promenade route amid fears that the sparking from the trams' trolley poles would be seen by German U-boats offshore. One of the fleet's star attractions was a brightly painted former illuminated car, known as the "Bandwagon", that toured the town for special events such as War Weapons Week and National Savings campaigns. It hardly needs saying that the Illuminations themselves, which would have effectively provided a giant "drop your bombs here" sign for the *Luftwaffe*, were cancelled for the duration of the war.

As well as training men and women, however, Blackpool also played a prominent part in the production of military *matériel*. One of its most distinctive landmarks was the enormous collection of hangars and sheds near Squires Gate Airport that together made up what was known simply as "The Factory". The Vickers-Armstrong plant opened in 1940 to build Wellington bombers (more than 3,400 in all) and at its zenith employed over 10,000 workers, with much of the work being farmed out to satellite sites such as Marton tram depot and the upper floors of the town-centre bus station/car park complex. The Marton depot, in Whitegate Drive, which had earlier been used by R.A.F. Technical Training Command, manufactured wings for Wellingtons.

One of the mysteries of the war is that, apart from an off-target raid near North Station in which eight civilians died, and a few dozen desultory bomb drops elsewhere, Blackpool escaped largely unscathed. The *Luftwaffe* was certainly aware of its military and strategic importance, and of the key role plated by the Factory. Indeed, German aerial reconnaissance maps clearly show the area around the airport, but the Factory was never successfully bombed despite four isolated attempts. With Liverpool 50 miles down the coast to the south, Goering probably thought his airmen had more important priorities. Indeed, the late Kathleen Eyre, *doyenne* of Blackpool historians, wrote graphically in her classic *Seven Golden Miles*: "...during the blackout [the] promenade provided a grandstand view of the vicious Liverpool blitz, with bomb flashes and dockland fires lighting the sky, and an incessant ack-ack accompaniment drifting over the dark waters."

Covering 530 acres between Blackpool and St Annes, the airport had been taken over by the R.A.F. Volunteer Reserve in autumn 1938 and later became a Coastal Command training station, and three new runways were constructed. The blocks of accommodation between the airfield and the sand dunes now form part of Pontin's holiday centre. The town's other aerodrome, the former municipal airport near Stanley Park, was taken over as a parachute training centre and never reopened as an airfield.

Blackpool was dotted with emplacements for anti-aircraft gun batteries and searchlights, particularly on the promenade and around the Vickers-Armstrong plant and the airport. The guns would come to life as German bombers, flying in from the east, swung south by the Tower to head for Liverpool. Air raid shelters and pillboxes were also constructed across the resort. The shelters on the seafront were built of brick with flat concrete roofs, and were located at each side of the various sets of steps that led down from the promenade to the beach between Central and South Piers. The pillboxes were not as numerous, but some survive to this day. There are survivors near Squires Gate Airport and beside the municipal golf course, near the site of the old aerodrome next to Stanley Park. There's even an unusual and little-noticed pillbox (built of crumbling brick, topped by concrete) on the northern parapet of the railway bridge over Devonshire Road on the approaches to North Station, which looks more like an old railway lineside hut.

The whole turbulent brew of wartime Blackpool was spiced still further by the thousands of holidaymakers who flocked to the Fylde Coast to gain some respite, however brief, from the war. The foreshortened 1939 season would have been a record-breaker if it had not been curtailed by the outbreak of the conflict, as visitors sought to enjoy a last hurrah before the war clouds finally descended. The last year of peace also saw the completion of several major development schemes in Blackpool, including the new bus station and car park in Talbot Road.

After initially discouraging holidays, the Government later changed its mind and decided they were needed to boost morale—and productivity—and Blackpool enjoyed a surprisingly buoyant Easter holiday as the "Phoney War" neared its end. In the wake of the German invasion of the Low Countries and the mass evacuation of British troops from Dunkirk, however, the 1940 Whitsuntide holidays were abandoned and special rail services cancelled. Even so, astonishingly, tens of thousands of visitors managed to make their way to the town by ordinary, scheduled trains. So many made the trip that Blackpool literally ran out of accommodation and some had to sleep on the promenade or even—perhaps apocryphally—the beach. Later that year, the summer "Wakes" holidays from the East Lancashire and Yorkshire textile towns went ahead as planned, and for the August Bank Holiday weekend the railways managed to run no fewer than twenty-nine special trains to Blackpool. In 1940 the Tower Company even managed to announce a fifteen per cent dividend for shareholders, and it was to be the start of several successful seasons for wartime Blackpool.

During the season there was a deceptive air of normality as holidaymakers in shirt sleeves and summer dresses sunbathed in deckchairs alongside the massive concrete anti-invasion blocks on the seafront. Motorists and bus drivers blithely weaved their way between the road blocks that punctuated their progress along the promenade. And the tourist invasion reached a grand climax in July 1945, two weeks before Victory over Japan Day, when the London Midland and Scottish Railway Company carried what it claimed was an all-time record number of passengers into Blackpool. A staggering (and very precise) total of 102,889 people arrived in the resort within twenty-four hours on the first Wakes Saturday of the 1945 season.

There were, of course, frictions between residents, holiday-makers and service personnel. In 1943, for instance, 3,000 boarding house beds were requisitioned by the Government at short notice and the visitors ejected, much to the consternation of the landladies. Tensions also arose between holidaymakers and visitors over scarce food supplies. And there was also some resentment among British troops, with their unflattering khaki uniforms and meagre pay packets, at the sartorial smartness, spending power and general *joie de vivre* of the "Yanks". But these cultural differences soon subsided as both sides came to realise they were in this war together, or not at all.

Then there were the evacuees—the "Vackees"—thousands of youngsters sent from the big cities of the North West to the comparative safety of the coast. In the first three days of war alone, about 37,500 arrived in Blackpool, clutching their gas masks and with each child carefully labelled, though within a year all but 2,200 had returned home. Many were brought back to Blackpool, however, when the blitz on Manchester and Liverpool began in late 1940. At one stage, more than half the households in Blackpool were being used as billets for evacuees or service personnel.

The final major group of incomers comprised the civil servants who were moved from London to improvised offices in 45 Blackpool hotels, including some of its largest and grandest such as the Savoy, the Queen's Hydro and the Norbreck Hydro. Within months of the outbreak of war, thousands of civil servants had made the trip to the Fylde Coast, many specialising in social security fields such as pensions and national insurance. This exodus to Blackpool was to have a lasting economic legacy for the Fylde Coast, which today still has one of the largest concentrations of civil service staff outside London; and, as with the early incomers, their successors are largely employed in departments such as Social Security and War Pensions. But the posting to "Whitehall-on-the-Water" didn't find favour with all the wartime émigrés from the sophisticated delights of the metropolis, and there were grumbles about accommodation allowances and the standard of their facilities.

Their pay was subsidised with what was described as a "billeting allowance" which later became a bone of contention between them and their landladies. On occasions, this disgruntlement boiled over, leading to small demonstrations in the town which were reported by the local press, along with letters of complaint by some civil servants. At times this correspondence became quite vicious; one letter stated, in effect: "If the enemy was ever to invade the Blackpool coast, the first people they would be met with would be some landladies, asking how much they would pay above the billeting allowance"! Someone must have severely rattled that writer's ministerial cage. Personally, I found the landladies friendly and helpful. They were particularly well-informed about what country you were bound for—despite the great secrecy that surrounded troop movements—merely by observing the type of overseas kit you had been issued with!

There were other points of contention, one of which provoked the so-called "Brolly Brigade" into uncharacteristically bellicose action. In the twenty-first century, the civil service unions often take a legitimately militant stance in defending their members' interests against successive Governments which have tried to make their tenure less secure and politicise their work. But in the 1940s the civil service was regarded as the ultimate in "respectable" employment: it provided status, security and stability and, in return, demanded rigorous adherence to the rules, which prompted the popular perception of a mild and compliant workforce. As in so many other areas, however, war revealed the underlying tensions in this strictly hierarchical system. And the incident which was to transform these desk-bound administrators into improbable rebels was an apparently inconsequential one.

Among the biggest enclaves of civil service staff was the one at the Norbreck Hydro, Blackpool's largest hotel, set on the cliffs about three miles north of the town centre. This sprawling, rambling pile is today known as the Norbreck Castle, and fittingly so, as its castellated battlements brood over the Irish Sea below like some medieval fortress. By the middle of 1943, though, the officials stationed at the Norbreck were becoming restive. While the larger hotels had been requisitioned for the war effort, many of the smaller ones remained open to cater for the holiday trade, albeit much reduced. During the holiday season, convoys of trams packed to the gunnels with passengers from these hotels on the north of the coast would sail past the civil servants as they waited to board them for the journey into the centre of Blackpool.

On July 10 1943, it all became too much and their frustration boiled over into direct action. After work, hundreds of civil servants marched out of their "castle" and across the promenade to the segregated tram tracks by Norbreck tram station ... and protested. They called for priority travel for war workers, and for the installation of a crossover which would allow trams to be turned at Norbreck, making it the terminus for some services. One contingent of the civil service battalion staged a sit-down protest on the tracks, while others stood defiantly before the trams, ignoring the tooting of their drivers. Dozens of trams were held up, and some drivers and conductors, as well as passengers, got off to remonstrate with them. The scene became fraught, with the civil servants decrying the fact that anyone should be taking a holiday while they were ensconced in their crenelated mock-Gothic workplace.

Eventually, the police arrived, and the protest was called off with a good old-fashioned civil service compromise ... the promise of an inquiry. The situation was investigated by the North Western Regional Transport Commissioner, who authorised more trams. The scene, with its almost Gilbertian echoes, naturally generated much mirth across the town, but it did once more expose the tensions between workers and holidaymakers.

Catering for both civilian and service sectors, the ballrooms and dance floors, theatres and cinemas of Blackpool were enjoying a boom time, as visitors converged on the resort to enjoy its attractions—no matter how briefly—before returning to the grey austerity of daily life. Churches remained open to provide solace for the lonely and dispirited, and hospitality and food were dispensed with Blackpool's customary gusto and cheerfulness. And it was the railway, despite its failings, that transported the vast majority of them to Blackpool. Indeed, Blackpool had been largely a creation of the railway almost a century earlier in 1846 when a branch from the Preston and Wyre Railway had been opened from Poulton-le-Fylde to Talbot Road (later Blackpool North). Hundreds of thousands of servicemen and women were transported to and from the Fylde Coast by troop trains or on ordinary services, and at Squires Gate there were sidings from the Blackpool Central-Lytham line to the Factory, traces of which could still be discerned until a few years ago.

The other main magnet for visitors was the Pleasure Beach, the 42-acre amusement park at South Shore created from what had literally been a beach, with a higgledy-piggledy collection of rides, in the early years of the twentieth century. Under its visionary managing director Leonard Thompson, the Pleasure Beach had enjoyed a boom time in the 1930s as he rebuilt and expanded it along the lines of an American theme park. He also commissioned the celebrated modernist architect Joseph Emberton to redesign some of its main buildings in the fashionable Art Deco style, and the fine, futuristic three-storey Casino complex, with its smooth, sweeping, circular lines, opened just before the start of the war. The outbreak of war put a stop to this headlong development but it proved to be only a temporary hiatus, and the park remained open throughout the conflict. The Pleasure Beach was particularly popular with United States servicemen, for whom it provided reassuring resonances of more home-grown attractions such as Coney Island in New York.

Despite the blackout and other restrictions, the Pleasure Beach enjoyed several successful seasons during the war, as servicemen, civilian workers and visitors all sought a little respite from reality. Amid all the gaiety, however, there was a pointed reminder that it was wartime, in the shape of a temporary R.A.F. camp on the less well-developed south side of the amusement park. There was also a second, less obvious reminder of war. One of the Pleasure Beach's earliest rides was Sir Hiram Maxim's Flying Machine of 1904, which still flies today using its original mechanism. The inventor designed the ride to promote public interest in, and raise funds for, his main preoccupation—powered flight—but he will probably be best remembered as the inventor of the machine gun that bore his name and which proved so lethal in the Great War.

All this gave a substantial boost to Blackpool's wartime economy at a time when rival resorts—particularly those on the south and east coasts—were struggling. From June 1940 the east and south coasts from the Wash to Sussex were closed to holidaymakers, and by mid-August this was extended from Berwick on the Scottish border to Dorset in the South West; only Brighton remained in business as a holiday resort.

When Arthur and I reported to the Blackpool headquarters, which were in a large hotel on the promenade, we were informed that (as we had suspected) we were awaiting embarkation overseas, allotted an hotel billet and given, at last, a yellow fever injection. We were then ordered to report to a certain sergeant each morning who would supervise the kitting-out process before our departure. This sergeant turned out to be Peter Kane, the distinguished boxer and lightweight champion from Yorkshire, a real gentleman who was devoid of the proverbial "bullshit". Every morning we would meet him for instructions, along with half a dozen other members of the squad for collection of kit, from various buildings on the town's outskirts. His instructions were always the same: "Let's get on the next bus." He hated marching. Our special job and destination were still being kept secret from us, although we already knew, of course, it would be in a "hot climate". When we arrived back at our hotel on the day we had been issued with bush hats and suede mosquito boots, the landlady definitely assured us that we were bound for West Africa. But even with her expertise she was unable to specify which part of that vast region!

All good things must come to an end, however, and a few days later, in the middle of the night, the transport arrived at the billet to take us, complete with kit, to a packed troop train awaiting at Central Station. We boarded in the darkness, along with personnel from other services. It was obvious that it was a special train transporting us to a port for embarkation, possibly to await the formation of a convoy. Once on the move, we made amends for our interrupted night's sleep but when we were awakened by the light of dawn, there was great speculation about where we were bound for. Owing to invasion precautions, all railway station nameboards and signposts of any description had long been removed. But it was obvious from the terrain through which we were passing that we were heading north, which was verified by the Scots among us, who assured us our destination was Glasgow. They were proved correct because two or three hours later we were lined up on the banks of the Clyde, waiting to board a Belgian troopship bearing the name *Leopoldsville*. The name was to prove one which I, and I am sure all who travelled on her, would never forget.

CHAPTER SEVEN
'Stew and spew'

IN BOTH world wars, as there was no routine transportation of service personnel by air, nearly all overseas travel had to be by troopship. Usually this was the most demeaning and undignified form of transport that human beings could be expected to endure. Heavy loss of ships due to enemy action had caused a dire shortage of troop carriers, which inevitably led to too few vessels carrying too many men. This resulted in merchant ships of various tonnages being converted to carry troops.

Such was the Belgian ship we boarded which was destined to take us to a "hot climate", as we had been enigmatically told. It was only a small ship of 5,000 tons and had been converted to carry 2,000 personnel. Its name, the *Leopoldsville*, was the only connection it could have possibly had with the eponymous Belgian monarch, we were soon to learn. Accommodation was allocated in the usual style, officers above deck and other ranks below. At first our R.A.F. section, composed of senior N.C.O.s, some being aircrew, occupied an area just below deck which although cramped was initially tolerable. On the same level, further along the ship, was housed the Army, with the naval lads being placed below at bottom level. (It always appeared to me that the Navy ratings were treated as though Nelson were still alive!)

Being among the first parties to board, we were able to settle back in what we assumed our allotted accommodation would be. However, we were then unaware that our transport would be moored alongside that Clydeside wharf for five additional days. During this period further troops would be boarding at all times of the day and night, continually constricting our available space. When we eventually started our "sailing up the Clyde", we did so with a complement of 5,000 bodies aboard. At least it was an enormous bonus to be moving, with currents of fresh air permeating those areas of packed humanity. There were no women aboard, apart from a handful of nursing officers, but already most men on the ship (at least those housed below decks) had been relieved of that part of their character they most valued—their dignity. To cope with the conditions, prefabricated toilets had been erected on deck but lack of space had resulted in a double row of door-less cubicles facing each other, so that when both sides were occupied, you experienced difficulty in negotiating the rows of bare knees!

Sleeping accommodation was such that it was only possible for everyone to secure a space if arranged in three layers—the top tier were suspended, Navy-wise, between beams in hammocks, the middle one were on palliasses on the mess tables, and the lower laid on the mess floor. I favoured a hammock, although initially I had to acquire the skills necessary to obtain a decent night's sleep. All the Navy lads below decks had long since learned these techniques, such as making "stretchers" to prevent the canvas sides meeting together, waking you in the night with a sense of acute claustrophobia. I soon learnt also that hanging above the chaos below prevented any opportunity to secure an "early night". On the contrary, you were subject to the continual bumping of your buttocks by those below misjudging the height of your hammock's suspension.

Early morning, however, presented the greatest challenge of organisation imaginable. It was a logistical nightmare to awaken the three tiers of sleepers, and to clear and stow their gear away to allow the mess orderlies to collect the breakfasts from the food galleys and deliver them to the mess deck tables. On most occasions the galley personnel were not always organised as slickly as those eagerly awaiting their food would have liked, and there were long delays. Here again the ever-present humour prevailed. Some previous unfortunate traveller, apparently perplexed by similar delays but not endowed with a great knowledge of English spelling, had carved deeply across the mess table the legend: "Why are we wi-ating?" This appealed to the R.A.F. contingent, who would, when the occasion presented itself, tunefully chant in unison: "Why are we wi-ating? Why are we wi-ating? Oh why, oh why!"

For the duration of the war, all alcoholic drinks were banned from sale to servicemen aboard troopships. As for the unfortunates who travelled on the *Leopoldsville,* this effectively applied to non-alcoholic bottled beverages as well. This was because the only means of buying them was through a small N.A.A.F.I.-type shop operating a policy of one small bottle per sale. This sales policy was academic anyway as the shop was only open for very short and irregular periods, during which the queue was always so long that the hatch was down before you ever reached it! Personally, I was never successful in these purchasing forays during the whole of my time aboard. Like my friends, I had to rely on refreshment from the galley's tea, coffee and cocoa stocks, and the awful tepid drinking water from the ship's tanks.

This first moving stage of our journey was to last just a few hours, for after leaving the banks of the Clyde we sailed up to the waters of Gourock Bay where we were to wait a further five days while a convoy was assembled. During this period, we were unable to discern much of what was happening around us as the December rain, mist and cold did not favour sightseeing from the deck. Instead, there were the inevitable, interminable card games below. We were aware of many merchant ships of all sizes continually arriving to form the convoy, along with the naval escort that seemed to consist of a destroyer and three frigates.

Apart from the abysmal living conditions, one of the worst frustrations was the complete secrecy and absence of information about what would befall us. This had been evident to my friend Arthur and me since our interview with the Group Captain at Weeton Camp, recounted in chapter six. It certainly conformed with the posters and hoardings of the day which warned: "Talk is dangerous" and "Loose lips sink ships".

On the tenth morning following our boarding, I awoke to the gentle swaying of the hammock and the hum of the ship's engine. At last I realised our journey had really begun. As I clambered out, however, and my feet made contact with the mess table below, before I had even made the mess deck I knew that I was about to be violently sick. Soon aware that the ablutions were already full, I grabbed some shoes and a jacket and managed to climb the stairs to the deck, only to find that the rails were already three-deep, mainly with the Navy lads. I emptied the contents of my stomach on to the deck where I stood. I had no alternative, nor did I feel any shame as this act was being replicated around me by dozens of fellow sufferers. It was bitterly cold on deck with a strong wind that made for a rough sea, so I decided to revisit the mess deck below to secure more clothing, particularly my overcoat. I managed, but rapidly returned upstairs as the scene below deck was of appalling squalor and sickness. Some unfortunates were so ill that they just laid in vomit.

It was difficult to make any progress along the deck in the conditions, which I am sure even the famously understated maritime profession would have at least described as "stormy". But I did manage to find a partly sheltered cranny, of which there are many on merchant ships, into which I was able to wedge myself to doze and be sick to my heart's content in comparative solitude. That evening, I awoke to realise that I had not eaten or drunk for twenty-four hours and that my stomach was completely empty. Unwedging myself, I gingerly made my way to the gangway leading down to the mess deck but, having reached the bottom step, I found the heat and stench overpowering. There before me on a mess table, however, stood a pile of large, dry bread rolls. I managed to grab one, before making a hasty return to the deck above and my previous wedged position, where I started to nibble at my roll. Previously I had never been able to induce myself to eat one of these rolls as they were baked on board with flour so permeated with weevils that it was impossible to pluck them out individually. So you had to consume them whole, with the consolatory thought at least that the insects were dead.

I spent the whole of the night dozing and nibbling, and finally consuming what proved to be a very nutritious roll, because at daybreak I was able to struggle to my feet and, although extremely cold and feeling weak, the nausea had receded. I even felt the need for a hot drink and some more food. With some difficulty, I was able to make my way back to the mess desk as the weather had not abated and movement on deck was difficult. Descending, the conditions were still grim but there had been an improvement since my last visit. This was due to the few fortunate lads who, being unaffected throughout by sickness, had been able to do some cleaning while assisting the recovery of their mates, some of whom had been transferred to the sick bays. Breakfast was available, after which on our own initiative everyone who was able set to with buckets, brushes, disinfectant and all the requisites necessary to get the mess deck really "shipshape" again.

Sea sickness being no respecter of persons or rank, there had been a complete communications breakdown between those below decks and the officers in charge of administration above. It was not until the following day, forty-eight hours after the convoy had sailed, that the first ashen-faced officers appeared among us. Gradually authority was re-established and inspections became the order of the day, principally the joint morning inspection by the ship's captain and the officer commanding the troops. During the period of sickness, I was constantly reminded of a conversation I had had previously with a fellow R.A.F. instructor in Blackpool about my overseas posting. Being an old-timer, he warned me that I would soon be experiencing a spell of "stew and spew". How right he was!

As we travelled further into the Atlantic waters, so the weather worsened and to those of us who were unaccustomed to the power of the sea, it was a sight that could only be described as awesome. For a couple of days and nights the convoy battled against mountainous waves that tossed around all the ships, regardless of their size, like insignificant corks. Such was the battering they received that one small French frigate travelling as escort on our port side was no longer visible one morning. This did not bother us initially as during the night, for security reasons, the vessels in the convoy would not be in contact with each other, so at daybreak they could be out of position. We were not to see the frigate again, however, and learned later from the grapevine that it had been so badly battered that it had to give up the struggle and seek refuge in port.

Inevitably, as we continued to travel south, the wind and storms began to ease and the sea became calmer. One evening, feeling the need for fresh air and the possibility of escaping "Far from the madding crowd's ignoble strife", as Thomas Gray put it in his *Elegy*—and before attempting the always-risky night-time climb into the hammock—I decided to seek solace on deck. It was cold and pitch-black, with no moonlight, as I made my way to the ship's extreme stern. Here there were a few bodies standing close together, gazing down into the sea at the lovely sparkling phosphorous colours created by the revolutions of the ship's propeller. As I joined them, the peace of the moment was intensified by the delightful sound of piano music wafting down from somewhere in the officers' quarters above. Whoever had gained access to the instrument was certainly a talented musician.

Before long, I became engaged in conversation with the body huddled beside me. In the blackness it was impossible to make out any features nestled within the turned-up overcoat collar. I soon learned, however, that my companion was a young matelot, who confided to me that he had not reached his eighteenth birthday, having initially succeeded in joining the Navy by subterfuge. It was obvious from his mood that he was feeling very sorry for himself, missed his mother and was deeply homesick. I was able to relate to him in many respects, particularly when he said that, like me, he had been an only child. As we parted after our close conversation, held in those unexpected, strangely intimate and almost pleasant surroundings, I was positive that I had helped to lift the gloom that bore down on his shoulders. Sometimes it's possible that a small incident can implant itself permanently in your memory, even though it occurs during adverse circumstances. This was a case in point, heightened by the extreme poignancy of the pianist including in his repertoire that gentle melody so beloved by my late dear friend, Victor—*The Folks who Live on the Hill.*

As the weather continued to improve, so conversely and paradoxically did our problems aboard increase. First, the personnel below decks were becoming ever more angry and agitated about the quality and quantity of the meals they were receiving. This was despite the many complaints voiced to the duty officers at meal times, and was particularly so regarding the R.A.F. contingent on our mess deck. They were mostly aircrew of warrant officer rank, some hailing from continental countries that were occupied territory, and all having experienced active air combat service. They were unaccustomed to, and incensed at, the appalling food and conditions they had experienced during the fourteen days they had endured so far, and considered they deserved better. This culminated in an almost rebellious atmosphere when they succeeded in obtaining a meeting with the Commanding Officer at the mess deck to discuss their protests.

The encounter did seem to meet with some success as, almost immediately, menus began to improve, with stew appearing on them less frequently. The stew was replaced by less monotonous canned products, of which more liberal helpings were served. As far as the latter were concerned, however, I later learned from my matelot mates below deck that this was achieved by cutting their own portions!

With the calmer conditions, it became obvious that we were now receiving the attention of the enemy's U-Boats. "Action stations" calls were becoming more frequent. On these occasions every section had its allotted station to which they had to report immediately, equipped with lifejacket and tin hat, and answer to a roll call. The areas were located on or below deck and could be changed on orders from above.

Increased activity could be observed among the naval escort vessels. On occasions they would rapidly sail in a certain direction, sometimes at a tangent to the convoy, and there was the sound of depth-charges being constantly activated, from different directions. It was apparent to us that the convoy's course was being affected. At one stage, the temperature rose to the extent that orders were given that all troops should change into tropical kit and put all their discarded clothes into their second kitbag which would be stowed away in the holds. No sooner had these orders been adhered to than the temperature dropped for a couple of days and left us all freezing! It seemed to suggest that we had travelled in a circle. Incidentally, I did not see my discarded kitbag again for two years until I was stationed back in the U.K.—when I must have been one of the few servicemen possessing two uniforms complete with greatcoats!

Most of our free time aboard was spent playing cards. For this reason it was vital that a card school was always at hand and, most importantly, that space was available in the crowded conditions to allow the four people to play. Therefore, Arthur and I recruited a more or less permanent school, consisting of ourselves and two others, Joe and Danny.

Danny was an ex-regular airman with a wide knowledge of all aspects of service matters. He was a character, well-liked and respected by all, particularly the younger element who sought his advice, which he was always willing to impart for their benefit. Hailing originally from the East End, he could always revert to expressing himself in the forthright vernacular of that area when he thought it was necessary. For this, we all had occasion to be thankful on at least one occasion. It was during a period when the convoy was subject to intense submarine harassment and "action stations" calls were frequent. We were taking part in one of these in a position below deck. Fully equipped with lifejackets and steel helmets, we sat on forms between the mess tables in what was a highly claustrophobic atmosphere, with the intermittent sound of activated depth charges. As usual, to ease nerves and pass away the time, our card school was in operation, along with many others.

Other men sat trying to read dog-eared books while their friends were quietly talking as they smoked. Then suddenly this nervous but almost tranquil atmosphere was shattered by an almighty, indescribable roaring noise, accompanied by an enormous physical shuddering through the ship. It seemed that for a couple of seconds everyone froze into silence, which was shattered by a lad's shout of: "We've scraped the bottom!" Instantly, this was followed by the loud and contemptuous delivery of a single expletive which whiplashed through the area—"C**t!" The monosyllable had been uttered by Danny, who still sat unemotionally dealing out playing cards. Without doubt his calmness and his immediate response to the absurd assertion that the ship had "scraped the bottom", although a coarse piece of invective, had succeeded in preventing what could have been a panic. It had made us all realise how ludicrous it was for a ship sailing somewhere out in the middle of the Bay of Biscay to be able to scrape the bottom! There were no repercussions after that disturbing event, with no official explanations, but then again we didn't expect any. It seemed pretty obvious to us all that a depth charge had been activated very close to the ship.

Soon after this episode, about fifteen of our R.A.F. contingent were ordered to attend a meeting in a ship's office with a Flight Lieutenant. As we were aware that we had all volunteered for the same special job, we were hopeful that at last we would be receiving some information about the future. Our assumption proved correct as the officer produced from a metal box papers relating to the bare outline of the project in which we were to be involved. We were told that this had been decided by the Government at the highest level and concerned the R.A.F. involvement in the four British colonies in West Africa: Nigeria, the Gold Coast, Sierra Leone and The Gambia. We would be disembarking at Freetown, Sierra Leone, where all concerned would be briefed by the Group Captain commanding the operation. Meanwhile, we would receive information and instructions aboard ship about the health situation and state of the infrastructure in these colonies. Although the information we received was sparse, we were pleased that we were now aware of a plan that might promise an interesting and worthwhile future after our grim experiences on board ship.

The *Leopoldsville* put into Gibraltar harbour seven days after leaving Gourock Bay, which demonstrated the circuitous route we had taken. Our contingent had been aboard for seventeen days. We were hopeful, therefore, that we would be allowed ashore for a short respite, but this was not to be. In fact, only one airman was allowed to enjoy that privilege and this only because he lived there! During our two days' stay at Gibraltar, it was disconcerting to realise that in view just across the bay was the Spanish port of Algeciras, an alien area. It occurred to us during our brief stay that it must have been a paradise for spying on the movement of British shipping through the two world wars.

We slipped out of Gibraltar harbour in the blackness of one night, this time as part of a much smaller convoy, our next port of call being Freetown. As we sailed ever closer towards equatorial waters, we were still subject to some "action stations" alerts but they were less frequent. Unlike previous convoys, however, we were never to experience attacks from the air.

Conditions on board did not improve as the temperatures rose and we faced the problems of keeping cool amid such overcrowding. Only salt water washing and showering facilities were available, and despite an issue of what was described as "salt water soap", you were left feeling very sticky after any effort to cool off. Although very few clothes were needed, some men also suffered from rashes caused by sweating. Also, of course, there were no cold drinks, and even bottled soft drinks were at a premium. In one incident, a member of the crew suddenly appeared on the crowded deck with a bucket of squashed lemons, with the intention of throwing them overboard. But those around soon stopped him. With the help of some sugar and the drinking water from the ship's tank (although tepid), a couple of bucketfuls of vaguely lemon-flavoured liquid were produced. Shared by the occupants of the mess desk, it could have been described in the circumstances as "nectar fit for the gods".

It was my first experience of sailing in equatorial waters, and there were times when I found it breathtakingly beautiful. On some evenings, a setting sun could colour the motionless mill-pond ocean a brilliant gold. Occasionally, thousands of small fish could be seen agitating beneath the surface, disturbed by something known only to themselves. I found flying fish particularly beautiful as they seemed to propel themselves out of the water for amazing distances. But perhaps I gained the greatest pleasure from the electrical storms that we would sometimes encounter in the evenings, with the dramatically coloured streaks of lightning flashing across the skies yet never, it seemed, any accompanying rain and sometimes even no thunder.

Occasionally we attended sessions in which we were given instructions and advice about the health situation in the four colonies. Much of the advice, although well-meaning, was doubtless meant to sound almost alarming: always wash fruit even before peeling, never tread barefoot on the ground, and never miss taking the various vitamins and other pills with which we were issued, particularly the anti-malarial tablets named Mepachrin, which apparently had superseded quinine. The very high incidence of sexually-transmitted disease was also emphasised.

Most of the advice and instructions were adhered to, the exception perhaps being the anti-malarial tablets. Mepachrin had the effect after entering the bloodstream of turning the whole body, right down to the fingertips, a distinctive yellow. We were informed that this would have no long-term effects on our health and would eventually disappear after taking the tablets. As my immediate friends and I considered that this assertion could not be proven, we decided not to take the tablets. We were never to know if our views were proved correct, but fortunately we did not contract the disease.

It was late one evening when we reached the end of our journey and anchored about half a mile offshore from Freetown. There were plenty of lights visible on shore, giving the impression of a busy town and perhaps even a bustling night life—a misconception of which we were later to be disabused. Our patience would be tested to the full because it was to be forty-eight hours before any disembarkation of troops would be started. It was then to be painfully slow as this could only be carried out by small lighters taking a couple of dozen men and their equipment to shore at a time. As always, however, the dullness was enlivened by periods of levity.

Throughout the daylight, small canoe-type boats would continually approach the ship, each heavily loaded with merchandise ranging from fruit to live chickens in cages, and propelled by a local trader using a paddle. They were certainly not welcomed by the officers on the ship's bridge high above, probably for health reasons. Despite this, they were occasionally able to negotiate their way to the side of the ship unseen by those in command, and would attempt to start trading. This was done by means of a basket being lowered at the end of a rope from above, and terms negotiated using notes and subdued voices. Invariably, before the order could reach a purchaser above, a hand would appear from a porthole *en route* and help itself to a bunch of bananas or other fruit from the basket. There would then be a heated harangue involving the seller and the buyer over who would be the loser, much to the amusement of the observers.

At times the exchanges would become so vociferous that they would attract the attention of the officers on the bridge, whereupon there would be scenes worthy of a silent film comedy if the orders from a loudhailer were not instantly obeyed. Shots would then be fired and, as the bullets hit the water around the boat, the trader would realise that the situation was now serious. His manoeuvres to rapidly increase the distance between his wares and the ship would result in his little craft rocking violently and the protest of the chickens on board. His hazardous departure would be accompanied by the vigorous flapping of chickens' wings and the loud cheers of the many onlookers.

As my friend Arthur and I waited in line to leave by means of a rope ladder into the lighter below, we reflected that we had been aboard that damned ship for a full month. Although the descent, carrying a kitbag and wearing small kit webbing and a large bush hat, was precarious, we made it with joyous alacrity.

As the lighter approached the shore, we passed a small fishing vessel. Hanging from the rail by one hand and waving at us with the other, a naked member of its crew shouted a welcome while simultaneously excreting into the sea. As I surveyed the scene with the *Leopardsville* in the background, I thought it was a very appropriate symbol.

It was many years later that I was to learn, almost as an epilogue, the fate of that ship. In a radio interview, the American singer Jimmy Roselli was questioned about his Army service. Jimmy revealed that his worst experience had been on board the troopship *Leopoldsville* when it was sunk in the Atlantic. He was rescued but hundreds of U.S. troops lost their lives.

CHAPTER EIGHT

Far-flung outposts of Empire

I am a Briton, bold and free,
I love my country well;
And proud am I, as all should be,
In such a land to dwell.

I glory in my country's fame,
The honour she commands;
But most of all because her name
For truth and freedom stands.

ON THE MORNING of every Empire Day when I was a young schoolboy in the World's End, we would sing this song with great gusto. On the platform in front of us would be the headmaster, seated with some obviously important people whose identity we would not know. In the background was always a map of the world, portraying the extent of the British empire, coloured red, which left little space for any other colonial hue. Towards the end of the ceremony, one of the prosperous-looking dignitaries would stand to deliver a speech glorifying the words we had sung. In reality, he had no need to do this, because we already believed in them and loved Empire Day—particularly the half-day holiday that would follow. We had not yet reached the great age of fourteen when we would be released to make our way into a society where we would learn about truth, freedom and racism.

In West Africa a decade later, as we stepped ashore from the lighters on to the firm ground of Freetown—one of the largest natural harbours in the world—we gained our first experience of the poverty there. We were immediately surrounded by dozens of children begging us to allow them to carry our kitbags up the steep steps to the road above, for a few pennies. In that heat, our resistance was weak, but they certainly earned their money.

Modern Sierra Leone had origins dating back to the fifteenth century when it was first visited by Portuguese traders. In the 1560s Sir John Hawkins, the English slave trader, dropped anchor three times, and Sir Francis Drake watered his ships there on his voyage around the world. But it was not until the later eighteenth century that Sierra Leone began to develop in its present form. The slave trade hadn't been one way: while 'black cargo' had been transported westward across the Atlantic, a growing number of black people managed to find their way back to the streets of London, where they were a source of cheap labour. Soon there were large numbers of destitute Africans in Britain, and a project was begun to settle them on Freetown peninsula. In 1787 more than 400 people—most of them black—set sail for Sierra Leone, and those who survived the arduous voyage made their homes in the colony. Later, it attracted free black people from

Nova Scotia and Maroons from Jamaica, who were the descendants of slaves taken from the Gold Coast, where I was to spend most of my time in Africa.

In 1792 the settlement of Freetown was established and Sierra Leone was declared a British Crown Colony in 1808. Located between Guinea and Liberia, it became the main base in West Africa for enforcing the 1807 Act outlawing the slave trade. It was to become a fully independent state within the British Commonwealth in 1961, but after a period of stable government, it descended into the now-familiar post-colonial cycle of corruption, government instability and ultimately civil war. Many of its most talented people, some of them graduates of the first university in sub-Saharan Africa, were forced to flee the country. According to a UN statistic, it was in 2003 officially the poorest country on earth.

Even as long ago as 1944, it was impossible to form anything other than a negative impression of all aspects of Freetown and its terrain. The sight of the infrastructure came as an immediate shock, with the open sewers running beside a few ill-constructed roads, from which earth tracks led into the shanty compounds. The general destitution among the inhabitants was soon appallingly obvious: it was inpossible to equate the conditions with the celebration of Empire Day in which we had been involved at school. Our R.A.F. contingent was posted to a transit camp in hills a few miles out of Freetown. During our journey on the R.A.F. vehicles sent to collect us, we had to pass some small shacks attached to villages *en route*. It was amusing to be greeted by waves from British sailors, already laying in hammocks on the verandahs while being rocked by the attendant "mammies". This was despite all the lectures and warnings on health matters they had recently received.

In his classic 1948 novel *The Heart of the Matter*, set in Freetown during the war, Graham Greene accurately captures the claustrophobia of the torrential rain and the oppressive heat and humidity of Sierra Leone. The book, based on Greene's own experiences as a wartime British intelligence officer in the colony, also perceptively portrays the underlying dangers of life in the capital, as well as the sense of ennui and isolation created by living in a remote outpost that could only be reached irregularly by sea through waters infested with U-boats.

But Greene, who served in the colony in 1942/43—I was there in 1944/45—was also captivated by the place. I am sure everyone remembers his first real experience of a tropical evening, the amazing cacophony from the thousands of wildlife species that abound in the trees and bush, as well as the continuous invasions of the fireflies. My friends and I experienced these pleasures when we ventured forth into the grounds of our transit camp on the first night after our arrival. In addition, we happened to be treated to the tuneful, wailing strains, floating on the air, from a distant village band of *Begin the Beguine*. Never since have I heard it played in such an idyllic setting. Continuing our stroll around the edge of the grounds, we were delighted to arrive at a building bearing the name "Salvation Army". Wherever there were servicemen during the wars, so there would always be a "Sally", catering in its inimitable way for a companionship so sorely needed for young men far from home. That evening we certainly appreciated their tea, "wads" (buns) and hospitality.

Although some miles from Freetown, we were soon to learn that the transit camp was not immune to the effects of the crime and poverty that infected the capital. For twenty-four hours a day, armed sentries were on duty at the gates and during darkness armed guards patrolled the grounds. Yet thieves would still regularly gain entrance to the dormitories and manage to steal possessions, including even kitbags. For these reasons each dormitory had to draw up its own nightly rosters to attempt to combat these problems. This operation had its difficulties as a couple of dozen beds, complete with mosquito netting, were not conducive to securing a clear view or vantage point along a dormitory and its sleeping occupants. Very few offenders were caught, and it was said that one reason was that they covered their naked torsos with grease, making it impossible to catch them!

Four days after our arrival at the camp, however, those of us awaiting information about the special job for which we had volunteered received some welcome news. We were told that the officer commanding our operation would be arriving that evening and we were ordered to assemble the following morning to meet him and receive information and instruc-

113

tions. This announcement to the twenty senior N.C.O.s was a great relief because the secrecy surrounding the build-up to the operation had been such that we had absolutely no idea of the job required of us. After the length of time that had elapsed, we needed to be given a job to do, to do it well, and to get it finished.

As ordered, we assembled the following morning in a small hall and were met by a Group Captain and his two assistant officers, both Flight Lieutenants. After being individually introduced, we were all seated around a large table and the Group Captain began to explain the project we were to be engaged in. First, he informed us that a new air force was to be formed, entirely independent of the R.A.F, and it would be named: "The West African Air Corps". It would be composed purely of black personnel who would be stationed around the four British colonies of the Gold Coast, Nigeria, The Gambia and Sierra Leone. Each colony would have its own station and facilities entirely separate from the R.A.F. establishments, where black personnel would be recruited, kitted out and supplied with uniforms. They would then be drilled and receive discipline training to military standards. After this initial training, they would be required to attend training courses in a ground staff technical trade. These would have to meet the standards of the R.A.F. courses in every aspect, including duration, quality and passing-out trade tests. These courses would obviously be the responsibility of us technicians.

We were further told that initially each colony would receive an R.A.F. complement of three officers and nine technical N.C.O.s. Black personnel, if suitable, could eventually be trained as instructors, and we would have the authority to promote them locally to N.C.O. rank. Also, local civilians would be employed in cleaning, cooking and office duties. It was also emphasised to us that this whole concept had been initiated by the highest Government authority, and it was implied that the War Cabinet or even the Great Man himself was involved. Apparently there was a great urgency for the whole project to be completed as soon as possible. This was because the object of the operation was to avoid sending R.A.F. technicians to West Africa in view of the need for more of them to be available for the planned D-Day invasion of the Continent, commonly referred to as "the Second Front". (This meeting took place in January 1944, five months before the invasion of Normandy on June 6, so time was short.)

The Group Captain had so much to tell us that it took us up to lunchtime, when he had to leave, so he handed the rest of the day over to his officers to inform us of the many details about individual postings to the colonies. Over lunch we were very enthusiastic about the scheme that had been unveiled during the morning. There was a consensus that it would be beneficial to everyone. Certainly there would be opportunities for many of the indigenous West Africans to improve their prospects and living conditions (we estimated initially there would need to be about two thousand recruits). It could also prove to be a very interesting and exciting venture for us, the instructors, while ultimately helping the war effort.

That afternoon, during our session with the officers, we received the details of our individual futures within the new organisation. Unavoidably in the circumstances, this was bound to generate some disappointment and even sadness among us because of our different postings around the colonies. My good friend Arthur and I would be separated: I would be stationed at Takoradi, a port on the Gold Coast west of the capital Accra, while he would be travelling on to Nigeria. Danny, our Cockney card partner, was to stay in Sierra Leone—a posting that could only elicit sympathy, as our experience so far of its dire poverty and crime had not endeared the country to us.

The detailed instructions and information we were given included further plans for transit to our allotted territories, and we were told that transport to the Gold Coast and Nigeria would be by another troopship, leaving Freetown possibly within a week, for Takoradi and then going on to Lagos, Nigeria. Finally, we were handed various pieces of literature to read when possible, including the constitution of the West African Air Corps. It was only on reading this that I first became aware of a different perception of the newly-formed organisation. I realised that it appeared to exist on the basis of pure and overt racism. How could I conceive otherwise upon reading one of the first written rules? This stated:

"The highest rank in the W.A.A.C. will always address the lowest in the R.A.F. as 'Sir'."

This rule, I mused, could have been written by my old adversary in Chelsea, Oswald Mosley, who had been detained for advocating a regime based on similarly racist distinctions.

I would discover many things over the next few months that would seem to make the white R.A.F. personnel "more equal" than their indigenous counterparts. These included a decree that the uniform issued to the black personnel did not include footwear; bare feet would be the order of the day for them "until they had attained certain standards". It was to be hoped that these were above the standards of whoever had composed the constitution! It soon became obvious that racism was endemic in colonial rule, varying in degree according to the people involved and the circumstances. I would always try to prevent or oppose it, at least as far as my personal influence extended.

While awaiting orders about the boarding of our troopship to our final destinations, Arthur and I, with some others of our party, decided to visit a bay on the Atlantic Coast outside Freetown. It was credited with having been an exclusive attraction for wealthy travellers in peacetime. Armed with packed lunches by courtesy of the sergeants' mess, we boarded an antiquated railway coach in the centre of Freetown along with some matelots. One sailor had his pet snake coiled around his fore-arm, which I suspected would not lend itself to a trouble-free trip. As the old steam train chugged slowly towards its destination, so the heat in the carriage rose. Fortunately, after about twenty minutes, the train rattled to a halt at what appeared to be a small station. Everyone seized the opportunity to leave the carriages for a spell, including the snake and its owner.

Seated in a row on the wooden platform were half a dozen local "mammies", displaying their wares of brightly coloured beans and fruits in large baskets in front of them. As our friend approached them with his snake, they all simultaneously screamed as they scrambled to their feet, in the process knocking the baskets and their contents all across the platform. Still screaming, they ran from the platform. In fact, we never saw them again before we left. Of course, the incident did cause some amusement among the onlookers—someone else's discomfort is often a trigger for comedy—but it also had a very serious side: the indigenous villagers in West Africa lived in an environment where reptiles were a potential mortal danger to them throughout their lives. I later witnessed the kind of tragedy that could befall them. An office worker at the camp had decided to visit his sick mother over a weekend, which involved him spending a night away in a neighbouring town. During this time one of his sons was bitten by a snake while playing outside the family home. His shouts brought his other brother over to him, who was also bitten. Immediate medical help not being available, they both succumbed very quickly to the poisonous venom. As it was the practice in the tropics for bodies to be buried within twenty-four hours, on the father's return he was to find both his sons dead and interred. I was to be really amazed at the stoicism and fortitude that this father demonstrated in the face of the cruel blow that fate had delivered to him and his family.

On arrival at the bay and leaving the railway station, we were surrounded by hordes of children ("picans"), some of tender years, determined to take possession of our towels and swimming trunks. This was so they could nominate themselves as our personal valets for the day, for which service their demands were just a few West African pennies. The bay proved to be an admirable location, certainly living up to its pre-war reputation as a tourist attraction for a well-heeled and fortunate few. It had a golden beach with palm trees and a shimmering, translucent blue sea with breakers that cascaded on to the beach, spreading white foam up to meet the trees. This excursion would prove to be one of the very few fond memories that we would retain of Sierra Leone.

A couple of weeks later, having said our fond farewells to our unfortunate colleagues who sadly were to remain in Freetown (including, of course, my good Cockney friend, Danny), we sailed round the West African coastline of Liberia on a troopship that was part of a convoy bound for Lagos. It was only a few days' travel to our first port of call, Takoradi, which was to be the disembarkation stage for our small W.A.A.C. contingent. We had once more to bid goodbye to the last of our W.A.A.C. comrades who were bound for Lagos, including my friend Arthur, my constant buddy since our first training days at Cardington. On my last day aboard we agreed to allow the ship's barber to remove all the hair from our heads in what was referred to back in my early World's End days as a "fourpenny all-off". Although the remarkable change in our appearance caused some merriment, we did set a trend on the ship and the severe haircut proved to be a hygienic asset during my time on the coast.

CHAPTER NINE

The Gold Coast: White Man's Grave?

ON LANDING at Takoradi Harbour—which consisted of two breakwaters enclosing a water area of 220 acres, with several quay berths—I was immediately and acutely aware of a different atmosphere and attitude to life in comparison with Freetown. Way back in the era of those Empire Days at school, the Gold Coast was referred to as "the White Man's Grave". This was not the description I would have applied during my wartime experience there. The R.A.F. catered for its white personnel with a military zeal that strove to eliminate any possibility of medical hazards, even sticking rigidly to a maximum tour of eighteen months' service in the colony. It was also my experience that the white civilians I encountered could all have been described as living in "extremely comfortable conditions".

Taking into consideration the plight of the native population—which included dire poverty and a disease-ridden society with no health service, leading to inevitable low life expectancy—I would have had to describe it, rather, as "the Black Man's Grave". We were soon to learn there were three important factors that affected life greatly in the area. These were an ingrained racism, "Ju-Ju" (of which more later) and,

121

surprisingly, what could have been described as a non-medical, self-inflicted ailment, known as "Coasty". This only affected the R.A.F. personnel, and its effects we were soon to experience.

Covering an area of 92,100 square miles—almost the size of the United Kingdom—the British Colony of the Gold Coast was sandwiched between the West African states of Ivory Coast and Togo, with Upper Volta (now Burkina Faso) to the north and the Gulf of Guinea to the south. Although a tropical country, it was said to be a little cooler than many nations within similar latitudes. Today known as Ghana, it was first visited by European traders in the fifteenth century. The constituent parts of the state came under British administration at various times: the original Gold Coast Colony (the coastal and other southern areas, including the capital, Accra) were first constituted in 1874. The colony and associated territories became the independent state of Ghana and a member of the Commonwealth on March 6 1957, though its political history has been somewhat turbulent since then, marked by coups and alternating military and civilian rule. One of the world's largest producers of manganese, it was also an important mining centre for gold, industrial diamonds and bauxite.

On the few miles' drive from Takoradi Harbour to the R.A.F. camp, we passed many bungalows and shacks with verandahs built alongside, under which workers beavered away with sewing machines, making a multitude of garments.

We discovered that a high-quality made-to-measure shirt could be produced in a couple of hours for just a few shillings. It was reminiscent of that old poem, *The Song of the Shirt:*

> And stitch, stitch, stitch
> Until the eyes were weary and red;
> A woman sat in unwomanly clothes,
> Plying her needle and thread.

We were also very pleased to find there was a distinct lack of that traditional military element of "bullshit" on the camp. But initially, combined with our first experience of the malady "Coasty", this informality was to be to our disadvantage. Having arrived at the camp during the evening in time for a meal and brush-up in the sergeants' mess, we found that our reception ended right there. No further billeting arrangements had been made for us. We were therefore without bed space, bedding or mosquito-proofing; in fact, we appeared to be virtually non-persons at the time. Apparently the senior N.C.O. responsible for troopship arrivals invariably went on a binge whenever a contingent of men was due in, and then took to his bed. Being considered "Coasty", he would quickly be forgiven and his misdemeanours would be covered up by his friends' making last-minute, very temporary arrangements for the unfortunate new arrivals.

(So what was the cause of this mysterious affliction "Coasty"? Anyone visiting the Takoradi area during those days could not fail to be introduced to possibly one of the finest lagers ever brewed; produced in an attractive tapered pint bottle, it was known as "Club Lager". Its smoothness, flavour and generally acclaimed quality were attributed to the water with which it was brewed. Its potency was such that it would have quite a morning-after effect on those who had over-imbibed. Its popularity with most of the camp personnel and the amount consumed, in my opinion, had much to do with the prevailing "Coasty" ailment. Certainly, months of regular indulgence would produce the effect.)

The next day we were able to meet the full complement of our Takoradi W.A.A.C. staff, who would be responsible for the entire Gold Coast colony. They consisted of three officers, five technical senior N.C.O.s and two drill instructors. The officers were the C.O. (a Squadron Leader), his deputy (a Flight Lieutenant)—both ex-R.A.F. "boy service"—and finally a Flying Officer, who was a former bank clerk. As we made up a total of ten, we were certainly not overstaffed.

That afternoon we received a major shock on visiting our future W.A.A.C. camp, situated on the coast about five miles from the R.A.F. base and aerodrome. It was, in fact, a derelict army camp. It had been vacated by the Royal West African Frontier Force, a black regiment which had been used by the British in campaigns in Africa, the Middle East and southeast Asia. But the length of time for which it had lain empty was a matter for conjecture: most of the areas around the wooden buildings and huts were covered by tiger grass more than six feet high. This was being attacked during our visit by a group of about twenty local grass-cutters wielding short hand-scythes, their rhythm being assisted by a musician playing an instrument that appeared to be a hybrid of a banjo and a guitar. We were told that the grass-cutting was a permanent job as by the time they had completed a circuit of the camp, it would be ready to be cut again.

Our problem was that the camp, since it had been abandoned, had become a breeding ground for all types of reptiles and insects. This was more of a problem for us N.C.O.s as we were to be billeted on site, whereas the officers would be accommodated in the main R.A.F. officers' quarters some miles away. It was readily agreed by the C.O., however, that it would be a few weeks before we could be fully billeted on site and during that period we would be stationed at the R.A.F. camp, visiting the W.A.A.C. base daily. Later in the day, before leaving, using the pidgin English we had acquired, we N.C.O.s fixed a deal with the grass-cutters' head man, the musician. We would pay one penny for every dead snake or scorpion they could display outside our future billet when we arrived each morning. It was to prove quite an expensive agreement as they exhibited daily a myriad reptiles and snakes of all sizes. But it was also reassuring because we were to learn that if even one snake was known to be in the immediate area, it became an obsession to make sure it was

125

eliminated. Those who have to share the domain of the snake soon come to respect its seemingly infinite capabilities, which include climbing and hanging camouflaged from trees, swimming underwater, digging itself rapidly into the ground, and moving with lightning speed when necessary for its safety.

It was two months before we were able to move on to the camp completely. During this time we had to work extremely hard to convert the buildings into the required trade work-shops, living quarters, cookhouses and our own sergeants' mess. We also had to organise and start up our various train-ing courses which, with our limited staff, would have been impossible without engaging in the delicate art of delegation. Here I was most fortunate. Although most of the first thirty trainees I received after they had completed their drill and discipline training were described as having been "recruited from out of the bush", there were two who had some educa-tion. One, Louis Adugu, was to prove invaluable to the run-ning of the motor fitting course. He had a natural engineering bent and I had only to show him once the theoretical and practical functioning of any mechanical or engineering part, and he would absorb it. Better still, he had the ability to communicate his knowledge to other trainees by using their diverse tribal dialects, which sometimes also included French. His companion, who somehow had acquired the English-sounding name of Edmondson, had lived in the capital, Accra. He had a more sophisticated air about him

126

than Adugu, but did not have the latter's educational abilities. He was bright, however, and—more importantly—was an experienced driver of all types of vehicles.

I made Adugu my deputy instructor on the fitting course and Edmondson my deputy on the driving instruction course. I applied for them both to be reclassified as Leading Aircraftsmen (L.A.C.), which would qualify them for increased pay and also the allocation of service footwear. Further, I made a recommendation that if they both proved efficient, they should be promoted to the rank of corporal. I was extremely surprised by the opposition that the latter recommendation provoked in some quarters, a reaction which I considered could only be motivated by racial prejudice.

We would encounter many unforeseen problems, particularly during the initial stages of the camp becoming operational. In the first few weeks we had between two and three hundred recruits living in what were known as the "African Lines", and being engaged in their initial drill training or "square-bashing" and/or trade training. On one of the first days, I was on duty with the Flying Officer and we visited the African Lines during lunch. There were two pleasant dining areas made up of waist-high brick surrounding walls with posts supporting thatched roofs. The interiors were covered with heavy permanent wooden tables and benches.

On this occasion, however, although all the seats in both dining areas were occupied and fully laden plates of food were visible in front of each occupant, no-one was actually

127

eating. Also our arrival was greeted by a complete silence. Adopting the usual system, I shouted: "Any complaints!" As there was no reply and the silence continued, I turned to the nearest seated person and asked: "Is there a problem?" To this he hesitantly replied: "We do not want chop cooked by men—we want chop only cooked by mammies." At this, the officer towering over him shouted angrily: "That is bloody stupid—now eat!" But not an item of cutlery clinked anywhere in the hall. This had the effect of infuriating the Flying Officer to the extent that he strode rapidly between the tables exhorting all and sundry in a stentorian tone to "eat, eat, eat!"

It was in the middle of the day with the heat at its highest. I was sweating and very apprehensive about the outcome of the unnecessary stand-off that had developed. We were just two men among a couple of hundred who were protesting on a matter of principle. Fortunately, on his last exhortation to "eat, eat, eat!", a couple of the more malleable men wavered and picked up their cutlery. This had the effect of breaking the protest and within a couple of minutes all the diners were tucking into their food, as doubtless they had been very eager to do. As we left the dining area, the officer said nothing but gave me a look that suggested: "That's the way to handle these people." He obviously did not consider that he had demeaned himself in any way, or ask himself whether he would have behaved differently if the diners had been white R.A.F. personnel. Nor did he reflect on how his demeanour had changed since leaving his clientele a few months earlier at his bank in Cheshire. But racism is such an insidious and pernicious scourge. A few days later, however, a team of "mammies" was introduced into the food production system, resolving the problem amicably.

Once being fully installed in our own W.A.A.C. camp, and as we had our own constitution and identity, we worked independently of the main R.A.F. station. We had our own medical officer, sick quarters and black staff, as well as our own transport comprising half a dozen vehicles ranging from the ubiquitous five-ton Crossley lorry to a purpose-built runabout with six passenger seats. This autonomy allowed us a very rare opportunity to try to understand the lives and tribal customs of the people of that part of the Gold Coast. Not only did we virtually live alongside them, but many had their homes in the villages surrounding the camp, having in R.A.F. terms been granted "sleeping-out passes". As staff, therefore, we were not subject to the normal R.A.F. "out of bounds" restrictions because we had to visit these areas when necessary, to investigate matters such as illness and absenteeism. These were almost invariably the result of having fallen foul of the local tribal police force after an over-indulgence in palm wine on one of the Saturday Nights Out that our black personnel enjoyed. As a result we would have to visit the local chief to pay the required fine to secure the offender's release.

It was for this reason that two or three of us staff would occasionally drive to a local village police station with a couple of bottle of beers on a Saturday night. We would sit behind the counter, ostensibly to check on the behaviour of our men, but actually to enjoy the kaleidoscope of entertaining little scenes enacted during the evening. These were all due to the various family "palavers" that resulted from over-indulgence in palm wine, which in some cases produced pure theatre. Sometimes the seriousness of an offence would result in an unfortunate being confined to a cell. This reminded me of Paul Robeson's lament in *Old Man River*—"…get a little drunk and you land in jail".

Living so closely with the black W.A.A.C. personnel, it soon became very obvious to us what power this thing they referred to as Ju-Ju held over them and the control it exerted over their lives. At first we were inclined to treat it with good-humoured tolerance, but with experience this attitude would alter when we realised the extent to which this malign influence dominated their lives. We would even see death re-sult from it. Our medical officer, placed in sole charge of camp health matters, was a young Irish doctor who was en-thusiastic and aware of the fact that being responsible for such a large black community would give him the opportu-nity to broaden his experiences of tropical medicine. Due to his constant need for transport assistance, I built up a rapport with him and shared a few experiences which inevitably in-volved the Ju-Ju influence.

One evening I received a phone message in the sergeants' mess from the sick quarters, reporting that an inmate was ap-parently possessed by Ju-Ju and running amok. Almost invariably the black personnel attributed ailments that befell them to a Ju-Ju spell. For this reason they wore charms around their necks which they would never remove unless forced to, in which case they would become visibly distressed. On this occasion I contacted the doctor and we both arrived at the sick quarters together. We did indeed find a state of chaos, with the black orderlies attempting to prevent an inmate from literally trying to run up the walls. He was promptly overpowered, allowing the M.O. to make an examination, during which he suddenly became curiously calm. Immediately the M.O. directed that he should be carried into the van and we should get him to hospital post-haste. As I drove to the "black only" hospital, which was in the control of the British Army, the M.O. remained in the rear of the van with the patient and gave me a running commentary about his condition. One of his last comments was: "We're going to lose this one, sergeant, but keep going as fast as possible."

When we arrived, he told me that the man had indeed died, but he thought the hospital would perhaps accept him as a "borderline" case. They did so, and relieved us of the formal proceedings and paperwork. On our journey back, I asked the M.O.: "What happens next?" He told me that he would be attending the autopsy the following morning at the hospital. I jokingly asked if the verdict would be that he "died of a Ju-Ju spell". He smiled as he replied: "The verdict will be that he died of chronic venereal disease," which was the cause.

In another incident that supposedly involved Ju-Ju, while acting as duty officer one evening I received a call from the guardhouse that a prisoner was going berserk in a cell, with the explanation from the guard: "Sah, he catch Ju-Ju bad." When I arrived at the guardroom, I viewed the prisoner through the inspection panel in the cell door and there was no doubt that he really was running amok. He was a big, powerful guy and there was no way that I was going to open that door! I contacted the "doc" at his officers' quarters a few miles away and he arrived a short time later. After reviewing the situation, he gave the order to open the door. Making sure that we were "mob-handed", I threw it open and about four of us overpowered the unfortunate fellow. Then the M.O., after a brief examination, knelt astride him as he gave the order: "Let him go!". It was an injunction that I was most reluctant to comply with! At the same time, however, he repeatedly smacked the offender smartly across both sides of his face, simultaneously shouting very loudly that he should "stand up!" Amazingly, this calmed him down almost immediately and in a few minutes he was quietly sitting in a chair in the corner of the cell. On leaving, the M.O. assured me that he would now be all right for the rest of the night. An hour later, though, I was recalled to the guardroom as the same prisoner had developed further unusual symptoms. This time, on my arrival, I found him stretched out on the cell floor completely motionless, though he was breathing.

Not sure whether this was in fact a ruse, and not wanting to recall the M.O. unnecessarily, I decided to make my own check. Obtaining a needle from a guard's "housewife" (an issue of equipment for repairing uniforms) I pricked his leg a couple of times but there was no reaction; he remained immobile. I decided that this was no sham and that I should phone the M.O. But the doctor said there was no need for him to revisit the patient as his failure to react to a needle was not abnormal for someone in his mental state. The M.O. said he would call in the morning. I wasn't able to find out how this case concluded, but in my experience any problem involving Ju-Ju always ended to the detriment of the victim. I did, however, catch a glimpse of this unfortunate a couple of times, making his slow, unsteady way under guard to the cookhouse—it was a regulation that all prisoners had to march to the cookhouse for meals.

I gained a lot of health and hygiene information from my association with this likeable young doctor during my visits to his sick quarters. We were always told that it was essential not to walk barefoot on any floor or ground, and though this advice was not always complied with by R.A.F. personnel, he was on one occasion able to demonstrate its wisdom. He had a black W.A.A.C. patient in his clinic with a small boil-type sore on his thigh. Eventually, on breaking the lesion open, the head of a tapeworm was revealed. Daily, the doctor was able to extract it very gradually from the wound by gently winding it around a small stick, and—in order not to break the worm by pulling it out too quickly—bending it over and securing it to the leg with sticking plaster. This macabre situation was the result of a grub entering the foot and growing through the leg. Needless to say, after that experience my feet remained firmly enclosed in slippers or plimsolls outside, particularly on the beach.

Trade test time

After six months of hard work and endeavour, the trade training courses of the W.A.A.C. black personnel were ready to produce their first trained technicians through the medium of trade tests. I was proud of what we had achieved in the motor transport training area. For teaching and visual-aid purposes, we had sawn through engines, gearboxes and axles, turning them into sectioned models. In addition, vehicle wiring diagrams were exhibited on table tops.

At the completion of our first motor transport mechanics' courses (M.T.M.), lasting three months, the first entry due for testing numbered fifteen. Although I was able to pass a dozen of these trainees through as Airmen Second Class, the very first test proved calamitous. I had arranged with Adugu that I would take them in alphabetical order for a preliminary oral test. A trainee called Aboagye was therefore the first, and I asked him about pistons generally and their function as part of an engine. "Sah, they make for up and they come for down and they make so..." he replied. This was accompanied by a rapid reciprocating up-and-down movement of his forearm. It was very hot and I was already sweating but I persevered, trying to elicit an answer that was more worthy of a three-month course in which technical information about the "Otto cycle system", with its succession of induction-compression-power-exhaust strokes, had been fully explained. But it was all to no avail, so succumbing to the effects of the temperature, I told Aboagye of my feelings in no uncertain manner—poor lad—his reply being: "You be true speaking, massah, but I can do it. I can try again." Unfortunately this was not possible as rejected trainees had to be transferred to an army unit, being engaged in general duties, goodness knows where.

Progress

At this time, in addition to the motor mechanics, our six-week driving instruction course with the assistance of Edmondson was enabling me to test and pass out on average six qualified drivers each week. Unexpectedly, the wireless and signalling section of trainees was proving to have the best passing-out results, with the trainees being able to pick up and operate the Morse Code system very well. According to Robin, their flight sergeant in charge of training, this may have been due to their rhythmical tribal music.

Airframe trainees also produced good results. This was entirely due to the Warrant Officer in charge of this section—an authority on the *Mosquito* aircraft (which had a wooden frame)—concentrating on that type of structure.

West Africa contained an abundance of all types of good-quality wood and therefore many skilled woodworkers. These chosen trainees were used to hone their skills on improving the infrastructure of the camp buildings to great effect. One building was converted into a fine church, complete with stained-glass windows, the latter being produced by the bottoms of wine and lager bottles being inserted meticulously into carved wooden frames. All interior work was handmade in mahogany, as there was a surfeit of that type of wood in the colony.

Twelve months after being installed in the W.A.A.C. camp, the training programme had progressed to a position where a regular flow of trainees was passed out weekly and posted on to R.A.F. establishments across the colony. This would achieve the object of reducing the number of R.A.F. personnel needed to be posted to the colony, enabling them to be diverted to the European theatre. That the operation had been viewed from above as at least moderately successful was proved shortly by a visit to the camp from a member of the Cabinet. This was in the shape of a noble lord who, accompanied by the Group Captain and entourage, sweating profusely, swept swiftly through the workshops in the heat of the day—and who could blame them?

Racism

I had succeeded in securing promotion to corporal for Adugu, although it had proved difficult. It seemed there was a reluctance even among our own people to see stripes on the arm of a non-white person, whatever his ability. It proved impossible, however, to obtain promotion for my other assistant, Edmondson, which was purely for self-inflicted reasons. Being an enterprising young man, he saw an opportunity to reinforce his finances by regularly siphoning petrol from the tanks of the five-ton Crossley vehicle during his daily driving instruction sessions, thus keeping the local taxi drivers supplied with an expensive and sought-after commodity. Inevitably, his misdemeanours were revealed by figures showing the enormous petrol consumption of that vehicle. I had no alternative but to place him on a charge, for which he was sentenced to six weeks' detention. Unfortunately, it was I who had to transport him to his place of detention, an army camp about thirty miles into the interior, a region which we referred to as "the Bush". On arrival, I could only describe it as a prison. Once inside the main gates, every movement had to be carried out "at the double", so after covering the three hundred yards to the reception building in the midday sun, along with Edmondson and an escort, I was not in the best of moods! Even while completing the paperwork needed to transfer the custody of my charge, I could hear the swishing of a cane and the protests of a luckless inmate somewhere in the building. So it was with some apprehension that I left him in their care for six weeks.

We also had a black member of staff named Mensah, who on being transferred from the Royal West African Frontier

Force had been promoted to the rank of Flight Sergeant because of his ability to train recruits in discipline and square-bashing. He had seen action in army campaigns and was treated with much respect, and accorded special privileges, even being allowed to keep chickens adjacent to his quarters. It was in relation to the latter that I once had to overrule his judgement.

Making a breakfast visit to the African Lines, I saw a group of trainees watching a box in a clearing about twenty yards away, with a lid held down by a small rock. It appeared that a snake had attacked Mensah's chicken coop during the night and made a meal of the chickens or the eggs, after which it had curled up to sleep to digest them. Meanwhile, it was reported, Mensah had put down the box, and the rock over it, and gone in search of a snake charmer! On being told that it had earlier spat at him, I guessed it was a hissing cobra, so there was no way in which I wanted to risk that getting loose on the camp. I rang my friend Jack for advice: he worked in the laboratory of the main camp's hospital and had a wide knowledge of reptiles. He arrived half an hour later, complete with bottles of chloroform. After crawling over the grass, dislodging the stone and opening the box, he poured the chemical over the still-sleeping and curled-up snake. It took two bottles to fully sedate it. He confirmed it was a venomous cobra, before putting it to sleep permanently. Mensah arrived back later without his witch doctor, but even so he was disappointed that we had dealt with the situation so efficiently in his absence. Perhaps we had been the cause of him losing a commission!

It was now drawing towards the end of our eighteen-month tour and our task was nearing completion. My experiences had given me very mixed feelings about the conditions I had witnessed in the colony. I certainly considered that we had been privileged in being given the opportunity to live with the West African people and gain such an insight into their culture. On the occasions when we had to travel through villages in the interior, the extent of the poverty and disease, with its preventable disabilities caused by the shortage of health care, was pitiful. In one village market a very old woman (hardly recognisable as such), with no feet, would crawl around naked on the ground, amid the dirt and dust, relying upon food thrown to her for survival. Yet seldom would one pass through a village without encountering a celebration of dancing and singing, accompanied by musical instruments. The stoical West Africans seemed innately content despite their sufferings.

Some also were able to empathise with the white R.A.F. humour, crude though it could be. There was the occasion when I was visiting the main R.A.F. Takoradi workshops and, meeting the N.C.O. in charge, he called to a black civilian fitter: "Poorman, come over and introduce yourself to the sergeant." He presented himself by saying: "Sah, I be Poorman, a very skilled West African engineer but a very poor man. Yes, sah, poor as piss!" Although in this case, the fitter was obviously a character, it was pleasing to see a mutual understanding between the different cultures, through the medium of humour. Would that this could always be the case!

A South African Air Force unit was stationed at R.A.F. Takoradi, although the Commanding Officer of the station was a British R.A.F. Group Captain, Wellington bombers being the operational aircraft. There was, however, little affinity between the R.A.F. men and the South Africans, who were more American-orientated, and although the sergeants' mess was shared, the two groups stayed apart and kept their own counsel. One reason was that the South Africans generally showed such a degree of racial intolerance towards the black civilian staff that they would not be immune to physical repercussions if they failed to please. Some of the "Springboks", I thought, would not need to take any lessons from my old adversary, Oswald Mosley.

Going home

I received the date of my posting back home two or three weeks before I had expected, but I was surprised at my immediate reaction. While I was naturally jubilant to be going home, my emotions were mixed and I experienced stirrings of sadness. I would sorely miss the unlimited expanse of sea, surf, beach and palm trees just a few hundred yards from the camp. This retreat during the hard work and tribulations that we had encountered in the formation of the W.A.A.C. unit had kept me and my friends physically—and sometimes mentally—healthy. But I would be glad to lose that constant, nagging worry which was the dark side of our camp existence, with the threat of disease, from so many quarters, always present. My paramount sadness would, of course, be regret at the ending of the many friendships that I had been fortunate to make during our time in the colony. This would particularly apply to my West African friends, who had assisted greatly in any success achieved in the development of the W.A.A.C. Transport Section. These would include Corporal Louis Adugu and L.A.C. Edmondson, the latter whom I had re-engaged on the completion of his six weeks' detention and who proved to be a reformed character. I was worried, however, that without my influence Adugu would soon lose his status as the only black promoted N.C.O. in the Technical Trades Section.

The feelings of regret that I was to experience at the prospect of saying farewell to my West African colleagues were greatly heightened when they learned of my impending departure. With Adugu acting as their spokesman, they invited me to be photographed dressed in the ceremonial robes of their local tribal chief. This I readily agreed to as I knew that it was considered by them to be a great mark of respect. The "photo-call" took place under the midday sun and, with the robes being of heavy velvet material, I was certainly relieved when the ceremony was completed! But the memory of such a demonstration of friendship and appreciation (along with the photograph) will always remain with me.

On the day of my departure, having said my sad farewells to the W.A.A.C. staff, black and white, I travelled the few miles by truck to Takoradi docks to join a troopship, this time a Dutch vessel named *Johann-de-Wit*. Having climbed the gangway and reached the deck, I turned to give a last wave to a few friends who had travelled with me on the truck, when a hand clasped my shoulder. It belonged to my old friend, Arthur! He had joined the ship at Lagos and, like me, had been the first of his W.A.A.C. unit to be released for posting back home. His camp had been in the Nigerian interior, so his experiences of the indigenous people of that area in the face of adversity were exceedingly grim, and possibly even worse than mine. They had certainly not endeared to him the ethic of the "Great British Empire".

Compared with our outbound experiences, our journey back to Scotland was to prove far less eventful. It was now 1945 and enemy activity in the Atlantic had been greatly reduced. Of course, the successful invasion by the Allies of the Continent had been completed and the enemy were a far weaker force than eighteen months previously. However, we did have on board a contingent of R.A.F. personnel whose troopship on their journey to Africa had been sunk in an air attack, resulting in loss of life. It was natural, therefore, that they would be apprehensive about their return journey on a troopship, to the extent that some would not sleep below decks.

As always, however, adversity was leavened by humour. In this case it was the recollections of a lad who described to me some of the events of that fateful evening when disaster had struck. He told me that after the direct hit, he had managed to climb up on to the deck above, to find that even though everything was ablaze, there was no panic. He stood by the side of another airman, both of them looking at the flames all around, when his companion took out a cigarette and asked him for a light. Despite the flames, he produced his lighter and gave him one! After this, with the deck's angle becoming ever more acute, he realised he had no alternative but to get into the water. About to remove his overcoat, he was advised by the same airman to keep it on as "the water will be cold down there". On jumping into the sea, however, the coat enveloped him but, while he struggled desperately to free himself, a small dinghy appeared with one person aboard. According to my narrator: "He was a big lad and appeared to be as happy to see me as I was him, and he plucked me out of the sea like a wet lettuce!" They and the others were picked up in daylight the next day and taken to Dakar.

This time we were allowed ashore at Gibraltar, unlike our confinement on board ship during our outward trip, before continuing our journey and eventually sailing up the Clyde—voyaging further into the eventful year of 1945.

143

CHAPTER TEN

Socialism in our time?

SPRING 1945 found me posted to R.A.F. Fazakerley, Liverpool. I had somehow escaped, temporarily at least, the attentions of Training Command, and was glad to be at a productive unit doing a useful job for the war effort. A scheme had been devised, so we were told, for fighter aircraft to be flown direct over long distances to combat areas. This would involve the construction of intermittent landing strips *en route* to those areas. We were therefore engaged in assembling small diesel engines for electrical charging plants, and crating and despatching them across the Continent, to provide electrical current wherever it would be needed.

Production was efficient, and although it was organised largely on factory lines, R.A.F. discipline was maintained, with working parades still the order of the day. This was particularly so of the first working parade after breakfast before we marched to the technical area, when the padre always conducted a short service. This would be preceded by a loud and very blunt order from a Warrant Officer: "Fall out, the Catholics and Jews!" This invariably meant a large number of people standing on the sidelines, excluded from the company of their friends who were being blessed in the ranks! However, I have many pleasant memories of

Fazakerley camp, not least of the sergeants' mess, which was to me unprecedented as all meals were served and cleared away by civilian waiters. The Scouse people, too, were so friendly, sociable and, when it was necessary, active in fighting for their principles and defending their rights.

By far the most memorable event, however, happened one evening when I was sound asleep in the billet. Some time after midnight I was tipped out of my bed by a large Scottish Flight Sergeant, who exclaimed loudly: "The bastard's dead—get over to the officers' mess!" In my half-dazed and confused state, I was not immediately aware of who the "bastard" in question was, but by the time I had dutifully climbed into my trousers I had been convinced that the epithet definitely referred to Adolf Hitler. I do remember accepting the hospitality of the officers' mess that night but further recollections of the hours immediately following the momentous announcement remain somewhat blurred. There were many V.E. Day celebrations held across the country during the following days, but people were aware that the struggle was far from over and those wearing uniforms could expect to continue to do so for the foreseeable future.

July 1945

During my stay at Fazakerley the great 1945 election was looming, and political party meetings were being held throughout Liverpool. Service people in uniform were allowed to attend these meetings as it was illegal for "mufti" to be worn anyway in wartime, so I was able to go to many of them. It was obvious from the political debates in these constituencies that the mood was emphatically in favour of a change of government. Amid the banter and humour, I remember the irate punter who in the middle of an animated debate sprang to his feet and, pointing an accusing finger, proclaimed in his loud Scouse accent: "Look, he's gone to bloody sleep!" At this, all eyes were directed towards the portly and rather elderly Tory candidate who had, indeed, nodded off.

Less than two months after its momentous party conference,[1] Labour swept to power with a landslide election victory, announced on July 26. Tories' hopes of a "khaki election" victory for the triumphant wartime Premier were dashed. Labour won 393 seats against the Conservatives' 213, and immediately set about making the fundamental changes to society that were to mark the 1945-51 administration as the most far-sighted, radical and successful, if not the longest, Labour Government in history. And all this was achieved against the backcloth of a country devastated by six years of war and facing an economic crisis as the United States summarily cancelled the Lend-Lease arrangements, which had provided Britain with the materials to keep fighting when it stood alone in 1941.

Hopes were running high, and in some political debates enthusiasts were even heard to declare: "There will be socialism in our time." Wiser counsels were inclined, however, to believe the statement associated with the former Tory Lord Astor, to "wait and see".

Once again, Training Command, through R.A.F. records, had evidently learned that some instructors had eluded them, so I and

146

others found ourselves posted back to where we had started, Weeton. My friend Arthur and I found we were once more together, and by this time we had both been promoted to the dizzy heights of Flight Sergeant. I was placed in charge of the hangar where the trainees completed their final practical training and Arthur was in the course control office. It was heartening to be associated again with those who had also been re-posted back, some of whom I had originally met while training at Weeton in 1940. Since then, most had seen service overseas in theatres of war as diverse as India and Europe, and they were very able and experienced engineers.

Inexplicably parked in the hangar were two pre-war vintage Bentley tourer cars, which I held in great regard as a result of my uncle's racing driver days at Brooklands. They had been there as long as anyone could remember and certainly did not belong to any serviceman. In fact, after lengthy inquiries, it became clear that their history could not be traced: they could have been donated by some estate at the outbreak of war, with no written records available. Eventually I received the permission of the officer commanding the course to use one as an aid for trainees during their practical training, with the proviso that its condition would not be impaired. During the running and inspection of the engine, it became apparent that major repairs were necessary, so to the delight of the instruction team I agreed for a complete overhaul to take place, at least as far as the availability of replacement parts would allow. Over the next few weeks, the engine was meticulously dismantled, with all main shaft and big-end

bearings, which were of Babbitt metal construction, being remet-
alled, rebored, recut and scraped by hand to fit. When it was finally assembled, the car had received an overhaul that would not
have been economically possible anywhere else. Yet it had also
been of practical, instructional value to the trainees and an interesting and enjoyable project for the instruction team. As far as
testing was concerned, although it was not possible legally to take
the car outside on the public roads, there was enough space on the
camp roads to experience the joy of driving such a beautiful machine.

With a little thought, I was able to come up with an excuse to
drive the vehicle each day, to the benefit both of the trainees and
the staff. During the morning break the trainees were unable to
have any refreshments as the technical area had no facilities and
the main body of the camp was too far away. I therefore arranged
to collect, in the Bentley each morning, a supply of tea urns and
trays of buns from the Sally Army and deliver them to the hangar
for the staff to distribute to the trainees, in their break, for the
knock-down price of a penny per cup of tea and per bun. But, I
used to muse each morning, what a menial task for such a machine when it had been built to circle Brooklands winning races
for a British firm!

August 1945

The events that took place during this month were to be indelibly
etched on the chronicle of mankind. It was on August 6 that the
United States dropped the first atomic bomb on Hiroshima. Its

fearsome power, which had been made possible by the splitting of the atom, razed four square miles of the city to the ground, with its effects felt many miles around that area. Only two days later, the Russians declared war on Japan, marching into Manchuria. On the next day, August 9, a second and even more powerful atomic bomb was dropped on the industrial city of Nagasaki. It was immediately obvious to the Japanese military that the devastation caused by these bombs was such that no earthly power could resist them, and the next day Tokyo broadcast an offer to surrender. Japan finally surrendered on August 15 after accepting the Allies' terms that had been laid down at Potsdam.

Autumn 1945

After the cessation of hostilities, Weeton Camp began to experience disciplinary problems generally among the personnel, particularly the course trainees. It was understandable that after V.J. Day most would be impatient to be demobbed and, as it was a Training Command camp, to be freed from what they accurately described as "bullshit". But inevitably it was to be a slower process than they wanted, and discipline would be more difficult to maintain as the experienced staff were released. At Weeton, however, there was a bigger disciplinary problem developing which unfortunately had a racial element. Many Jamaicans had been posted to Weeton for trade training courses, following widescale recruitment exercises during hostilities. They shared the general desire to be free from service life and, like their white counterparts, were not enamoured of any attempts to enforce strict discipline. Therefore standards of discipline were falling. Gone, of course, were the days of 1940 when the ex-Indian Army officer and his enthusiastic N.C.O.s kept strict disciplinary control of us poor minions—from billet to parade ground—so it was very difficult for technical N.C.O.s, who themselves were mostly awaiting release, to maintain course discipline.

This was most evident during a working parade one morning, held in miserable, rainy conditions before marching to the technical area to start work. Arthur and I, being on parade duty, were fronting a couple of hundred trainees. On calling the assembly to attention, I noticed a large Jamaican in the front rank at the extreme left, still standing with his coat collar turned up and with his hands firmly in his pockets. Arthur, who was quite close to the man, told him to take his hands out of his pockets and stand to attention. As this order was completely ignored, it was obvious that it had become a deliberately confrontational incident. In an attempt to maintain discipline in the circumstances, Arthur ordered a couple of men to fall out and take the offender to the guardroom. Actually it took four men to accomplish this and he was carried spread-eagled to the guardroom while I got everyone to work. As the six people (including Arthur) entered the room, they were joined by a Jamaican Warrant Officer who, having seen a fellow countryman being handled in such an undignified manner, wanted to register his displeasure.

For attacking a senior N.C.O. and fellow airmen, the offender could have faced court-martial charges. However, the protesting Warrant Officer—a redundant aircrew member having to re-muster to a ground staff post—naturally felt an affinity with his fellow Jamaican trainee, and insisted on a meeting with the Commanding Officer as he considered there had been racial undercurrents to the incident. In the event of possible court-martial charges being laid, a review of evidence had to be held, to which Arthur was called as a chief witness. After giving his evidence, he had to answer questions in an atmosphere that, according to him, was so hostile that he had the impression it was he who was being charged. Subsequently no court-martial charges were laid and no action was taken.

Naturally Arthur was furious at the outcome as, from his point of view in trying to maintain discipline, it was indirectly implied that he had acted with racial motives. It certainly didn't encourage him to maintain any enthusiasm for implementing disciplinary procedures in the future. In order to preserve good relations with the embassies and high commissions in London, it seemed, the policy was that any incidents which could be construed as being racially motivated should be played down or avoided.

By this time the more experienced instructors were increasingly becoming eligible for release under the demobilisation programme. This caused extra problems but we were still able to maintain our quota of trained fitters weekly through their final hangar stages. For me, it was to prove a memorable milestone as it was the month when my daughter was born. Ironically, I had to collect her and my wife from her birthplace at Brocket Hall in Welwyn Garden City, Hertfordshire, the former home of Lord Brocket, who was an admirer of Hitler and supporter of Oswald

Mosley. Since both he and Mosley had been interned, the handsome mansion had been commandeered as a maternity hospital for London mothers throughout the Blitz. As the oil paintings of Nazi leaders still adorned the walls, Dolly had the unwanted distinction of von Ribbentrop peering down upon her during her confinement!

It was in May 1946, by then based at Uxbridge, that I was released from the R.A.F and, like thousands of others, I possessed little more after six years than a demob suit and some new-found independence. Arthur was demobbed with me and, having completed most of our service together, our friendship was to continue for many more years. With no job, no property, very little money and those very important career-building years between twenty-four and thirty now behind me, the prospects for caring for a wife and young family could have been better. But of course with a new Labour Government in power, and the words "socialism in our time" ringing in my ears, I ventured forth into what could possibly become, in Lloyd George's famous phrase, "a fit country for heroes to live in".

There was only one hope of obtaining a house, and that was through a local council as house-building had stagnated during the war years. Competition was stiff for these homes as many discharged servicemen were applying, including ex-officers. After a few weeks I did manage to move into a council house with Dolly and the two small children in the London suburb of South Ruislip. Unfortunately, the local council almost immediately yanked the weekly rent up due, it said, to the "actions of central government". Residents were naturally aggrieved and quickly formed a tenants' association, electing me secretary. While canvassing the estate for signatures on a protest petition, a former captain was told to "watch that new secretary as he has a twenty pounds-a-week position" (which at the time was an exceptionally high salary). To this the canvasser retorted: "Thanks, I'll tell his wife later as she knows nothing about it." Neither would I as I had not yet started a permanent job!

Initially steering clear of political parties, I developed an interest in the trade union movement, joining the local branch of the Amalgamated Union of Engineering Workers (A.E.U.). It was here that I was pleased to make the acquaintance of a well-known trade unionist, Wal Hannington, who would later become a good friend. In my teens I had read his book *Unemployed Struggles,* and had admired the socialist principles he had set out in it. During the early 1930s he had been involved in the unemployed workers' marches from the North of England to London—the "hunger marches". At the time he was our A.E.U. District Secretary but he had previously held the higher position of National Organiser. His problem was that as a member of the Communist Party he had been dismissed due to a new union rule that said no member of the C.P. could hold any position or office in the union. This was not considered to be democratic by many members, particularly as there were two Communist M.P.s at the time: Willie Gallacher of Fife and Phil Piratin of Stepney. Eventually democracy prevailed and the rule was rescinded, allowing Wal to be elected to the lower position of District Secretary.

Judged by any standards, Wal was a fine orator and wordsmith, and he composed an "Initiatory Address" for union branches. This document could be read out by the chairman of branches to new members at their first meeting. I found it an inspirational and rousing socialist statement, particularly the final stanza, which read:

> May you long give service to the cause of trade unionism. May you live to see the day when the unity of the workers becomes so strong that we can end the system which creates unemployment and poverty in the midst of plenty and replace it with a just and equitable one, which will ensure a full and happy life to all who render useful service in society. May you honour and cherish that ideal and strive for its accomplishment. Permit me now, in the name of the officers and members of this union, to extend to you the hand of trade union brotherhood and warmly welcome you into our ranks.

Through him I was to meet the leader of the mineworkers' union, Arthur Horner, a fiery Welshman who lived in Wembley at that time. Both were committed Leninists, always generous with their praise of the former Soviet leader's doctrines, and his portraits prominently adorned the walls of both their sitting rooms. In fact, Arthur had chaired meetings attended by Lenin when he had visited London before the 1917 revolution.

As we were entering another new era, with fascism and racism soundly defeated but at such enormous cost, one could have been excused for expecting some relaxation of the threat from that particular menace. This was not to be, however, because as early as February 1948 Oswald Mosley founded a new organisation, Union Movement, and tried to make a comeback. "It is the task of a new movement to build where the old parties have destroyed," he declared. "...We will create a third empire after they have lost two empires." This time he was peddling his poison principally against black people who were most vulnerable to racist attacks. There was still a good deal of latent anti-Semitism in the movement, though it was rarely expressed publicly, but during the 1950s its main focus of activity shifted from the East End to the area of Kensington north of Notting Hill, the main centre for West Indian immigration in London. At that time there were no restrictions on immigration from the Commonwealth and there was considerable unemployment in the West Indies. As happened during the 1930s, many of Mosley's meetings ended in violence, and the friction came to a head in the summer of 1958 when there were street fights between gangs of Afro-Caribbean youths and white "Teddy Boys".

Mosley's policy was to expel all coloured people, except students, from Britain, but when he stood as parliamentary candidate for North Kensington in the 1959 general election he lost his deposit for the first time in his career, receiving just eight per cent of the vote. He had been confident almost of winning, according to his anti-racist son, Nicholas. The last time he stood for Parliament was in 1966 when he contested Shoreditch, polling less than five per cent of the votes. After this he gave up the leadership of Union Movement and retired from politics, though he never surrendered his grandiose dream of a great combined nation of Europe-with-Africa. This Euro-African power bloc would be stronger than either the United States or the Warsaw Pact. (Unsurprisingly, it would be Europe that would be running large tracts of Africa, rather than the reverse, through a democratically elected parliament and executive.)

While all this was happening, some even more virulent racists were emerging who claimed that the Holocaust, concentration camps and the Warsaw Ghetto had never existed and were the inventions of politically and religiously motivated propagandists! So, in accordance with the truism that "Evil can only exist when good people do nothing", there was to be a need for more action. But, as I concluded in the first volume of these memoirs, that is another story.

NOTE

[1] In the same Blackpool hall where only weeks earlier R.A.F. recruits had been doing their gymnastic exercises, Labour Party members gathered in May 1945 for a conference that would shape the future of post-war Britain. Barely a fortnight after V.E. Day, the sumptuous surroundings of the Empress Ballroom at the Winter Gardens were to become the setting for a political drama as delegates converged on my old haunts for the conference, in an atmosphere awash with euphoria.

Of all the items on the agenda—many concerned with post-war reconstruction—one stood out: the question of continuation of the wartime coalition with Churchill. Before the conference, the Prime Minister had offered Attlee the choice of an immediate election or a continuation of the coalition until the war against Japan was over. Both he and Attlee wanted Labour to stay in the coalition until the end of the war in the Pacific, but conference delegates had other ideas. A succession of young parliamentary candidates strode to the rostrum—many (quite improperly) wearing military uniform—and demanded an end to the alliance and an early start on building the new post-war Britain. There had not been a general election for a decade, they pointed out. Major Denis Healey, Lieutenant James Callaghan and Captain Roy Jenkins were among the most prominent.

In the event, on the recommendation of the National Executive Committee, the conference voted in favour of staying in the coalition until the end of the present Parliament in October but no later. Churchill would have nothing of this compromise. While Labour was still gathered in Blackpool, he went to Buckingham Palace to submit his resignation, formed a caretaker government and called an election for July 5, a date that was revealed during the conference. To allow the service vote to be counted, the result would be announced three weeks later. The war in the Far East had been expected to last several more months; in fact, Hiroshima and Nagasaki would bring the conflict to a conclusion within three weeks of Labour's triumph being announced.

BIBLIOGRAPHY

Beckett, Francis, *Clem Attlee* (Richard Cohen Books, 1997)

Benn, Tony, *The Benn Diaries* (ed. Ruth Winstone, Arrow Books, 1994)

Cross, Colin, *The Fascists in Britain* (Barrie and Rockliff, 1961)

Eyre, Kathleen, *Seven Golden Miles* (Dalesman, 1989)

Fienburgh, Wilfred, *Twenty-five Momentous Years* (Odhams, 1955)

Foster, David, *Excursions into Fylde History* (Hendon Publishing)

Goldberg, Alf, *World's End for Sir Oswald* (The Book Guild, 1999)

McLoughlin, Barry, *Railways of Blackpool and the Fylde* (Silver Link, 1996 and 1999)

Palmer, S. and Turner, B., *Blackpool by Tram* (Palmer & Turner, 1968)

Taylor, J.W.R. and Moyes, P.J.R., *Pictorial History of the R.A.F.*, Volume 2 (Ian Allan, 1969)

Turner, B. and Palmer, S., *The Blackpool Story* (Palmer & Turner, 1976)

Walton, John K., *Blackpool* (Edinburgh University Press/Carnegie Publishing, 1998)

Walton, John K., *The Blackpool Landlady: A Social History* (Manchester University Press, 1978)